Sea View Camping
WALES

Printed in Wales by:

STEPHENS & GEORGE

6 842 430 000

Derived from a guide first published in Great Britain by Brian M. Leahy, 2006. Reprinted 2007.
Republished 2008 and 2010 by Vicarious Books Ltd.
This variant published 2014.

Vicarious Books, 62 Tontine Street, Folkestone, Kent, CT20 1JP. Tel: 0131 2083333
www.VicariousBooks.co.uk

Author: Andy Clarke

Editors: Chris Doree, Pami Hoggatt, Caroline Stacey and Meli George

Design and artwork by: Chris Gladman Design Tel: 07745 856652

Front cover
Main picture: Aberafon.
Small pictures: Bryn Bach, Caerfai Bay and Tyddyn Du.

Back cover
Small pictures: Treheli Farm and Beach at Mwnt.

What's inside this unique guide?

This unique guide shows and tells you about the sea view campsites around Wales. There are campsites alongside private pebble beaches, nestled at the foot of Iron Age hill forts and plenty surrounded by lush green pastures.

Within this guide there is every type of campsite from family focussed holiday parks to farmers' fields down dirt tracks and laid back camping where you can sing around a camp fire. All you have to do is decide upon where you want to go and be ready for a fantastic time as you explore the hills, mudflats, cliffs and caves.

Andy Clarke embarked on a series of inspection tours searching out potential sea view campsites along the way. His brief was to include every campsite with a good sea view, and as far as is possible that has been done. The result is that you are now reading the most comprehensive compilation of sea view campsites located around Wales.

To help you make informed choices, each listing includes a photo and a description of the sea view. The quality of the facilities and amenities are not formally judged, but are listed and commented upon. Where appropriate the local area and attractions are mentioned. Beach access is normally easy, but this is discussed as necessary. In addition, the location of the nearest pub, shop, beach and slipway is provided to further assist you.

When available the campsite's own website address is provided. Should any updates or amendments be made known to us, these will be published at
http://www.vicariousbooks.co.uk/guide_updates.shtml

Beach at Trefalen Farm

HOW TO USE THIS GUIDE

Campsite location – The numbers printed on the map on page 15 identify and locate each campsite. The campsites are listed geographically and in map number order on pages 8-9. Use this list to find the map reference number, the campsite name and the page number of the listing. Page numbers can also be found by campsite name using the alphabetical index starting on page 72.

Entry explanation

1 **Campsite name**

2 **Campsite map reference number**

3 **Campsite address and phone number**

4 **Campsite website, where available**

5 **Photo of the sea view from the campsite**

6 **Units accepted by campsite**

   Å   *Tent*

   🚐   *Touring caravan*

   🚐   *Motorhome*

   🚐   *Large vehicles* - Motorhomes/Caravans/5th Wheels. Campsites were checked for accessibility and the owners/managers were asked whether large vehicles were accommodated on the site. Where highlighted, access should be possible for competent and experienced drivers. Most campsites only accept very large vehicles with advanced bookings and we insist that you discuss access and pitch availability with campsite staff before arrival.

   🚐   *Holiday accommodation for hire* – Many of the campsites in this guide have other accommodation for hire (i.e. static caravans, holiday homes, chalets, or lodges). This accommodation has not been inspected and may not have the sea view described in the listing.

7 **Description** – An unbiased description is given of the site and the sea view. The strengths or weaknesses and appeal of the site are provided. Further useful information is also given.

8 **Symbols** – The following symbols are used to identify the size and facilities of the site. All sites have a water tap and a toilet disposal point unless otherwise stated. Facility only available when highlighted.

   NA   Number of acres, where known

   NP   Number of pitches

   ⚡   Electricity available and amperage, where known

   🔌   Level pitches

   🔌   All season/hardstanding pitches

   WC   Toilets

   ♿   Disabled toilets

   🚿   Showers

   🛁   Family bathroom/shower room

   🍽️   Dishwashing facilities

   🧺   Laundry

   MG   Motorhome wastewater disposal

   MB   Motorhome toilet waste disposal

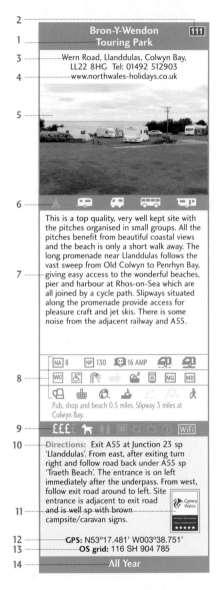

2 · · · · · ·
1 · · · · · ·
3 · · · · · ·
4 · · · · · ·
5 · · · · · ·
6 · · · · · ·
7 · · · · · ·
8 · · · · · ·
9 · · · · · ·
10 · · · · · ·
11 · · · · · ·
12 · · · · · ·
13 · · · · · ·
14 · · · · · ·

Bron-Y-Wendon Touring Park — [111]

Wern Road, Llanddulas, Colwyn Bay, LL22 8HG Tel: 01492 512903
www.northwales-holidays.co.uk

This is a top quality, very well kept site with the pitches organised in small groups. All the pitches benefit from beautiful coastal views and the beach is only a short walk away. The long promenade near Llanddulas follows the vast sweep from Old Colwyn to Penrhyn Bay, giving easy access to the wonderful beaches, pier and harbour at Rhos-on-Sea which are all joined by a cycle path. Slipways situated along the promenade provide access for pleasure craft and jet skis. There is some noise from the adjacent railway and A55.

NA 8 NP 130 ⚡ 16 AMP
WC MG MB
Pub, shop and beach 0.5 miles. Slipway 3 miles at Colwyn Bay.

£££

Directions: Exit A55 at Junction 23 sp 'Llanddulas'. From east, after exiting turn right and follow road back under A55 sp 'Traeth Beach'. The entrance is on left immediately after the underpass. From west, follow exit road around to left. Site entrance is adjacent to exit road and is well sp with brown campsite/caravan signs.

GPS: N53°17.481' W003°38.751'
OS grid: 116 SH 904 785

All Year

The following symbols identify amenities that are either on site or nearby as indicated. The facilities have not been tested and charges may apply.

- ⊞ Pub/bar
- ⛪ Shop
- ☕ Beach
- ⚓ Slipway
- 🏊 Indoor or outdoor swimming pool
- 🛝 Children's play area
- 🚶 Footpath

9 Information Symbols

Cost – The cost of the campsite is indicated by the £ symbols. All prices are based on two people in one caravan or motorhome with electric during August. Prices are offered as a guideline only and should always be confirmed in advance.

£	Up to £10 per night
££	£10-17 per night
£££	£17-35 per night
££££	£35 or more per night

🐕 Many campsites allow dogs on site, indicated by the dog symbol, but confirmation must always be sought in advance that your dog(s) can be accommodated. Many campsites charge extra for dogs, there may be a limit on the number of dogs allowed on site, and some sites specify the type of units that dogs can be accommodated in. Some sites also have breed restrictions, so always check your breed is permitted before arrival. Campsite owners and other holidaymakers expect dogs to be kept quiet and under control, and usually on a lead, at all times. Dogs must be exercised in appropriate areas, or offsite, and all mess must be cleared in a responsible fashion. In addition, it is advised that you never leave your dog unattended.

👫 This symbol refers to adult only campsites. No person under the age of 18 will be admitted.

Ⓜ This symbol refers to member only campsites. Generally these belong to either the Camping and Caravanning Club or the Caravan Club and a valid membership is required to stay, though it may be possible to join at reception. The name of the club is usually indicated in the title of the campsite. CS and CL sites are also for members only.

CS (Certified Sites) - These sites are for Camping and Caravanning Club members only. These are small sites, restricted to five caravans or motorhomes, plus tents space permitting.

CL (Certified Locations) - These sites are for Caravan Club members only. These are small sites, restricted to five caravans or motorhomes.

ⓘ Internet available (charges may apply).

WiFi WiFi available (charges may apply).

10 Directions – Directions are provided. Please note that many campsites near the sea are down narrow lanes with passing places.

11 Awards – Cymru Wales awarded star ratings.

12 GPS Coordinates – Coordinates are presented in true GPS format. Our office, for example, is located at N51˚04.895' E001˚10.978'. You may need to select this format in your navigator's menu. Coordinates were recorded at the site entrance, or sometimes the approach road/driveway, to prevent navigator error. We have provided directions that should be suitable for most vehicles but your navigator may not, so ensure that you check the route against a map and our directions. Please note that postcodes often do not provide accurate destinations when used with satellite navigators.

13 OS grid references – The six figure grid references provided refer to locations on the Ordinance Survey Landranger 1:50,000 sheet map series. The first three numbers and the two letters refer to the map identification code. The remaining numbers create a six-digit grid reference. Unlike the GPS coordinates, these will locate the campsite rather than the entrance.

14 Opening dates – Opening dates change year to year and are given as an indication only, please check with the campsite before arrival.

15 Advanced booking – You will need to contact the individual campsites to make advanced bookings, especially if you are planning a visiting during the summer holidays or other peak periods.

Abbreviations
mins = minutes   sp = signposted

Vicarious Books

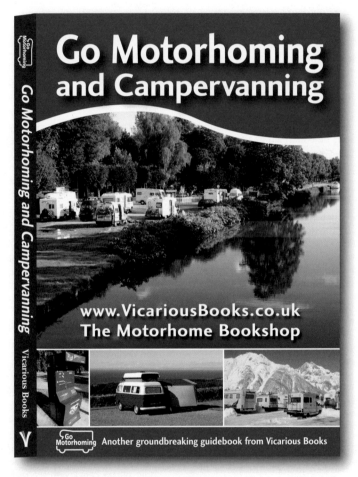

Dwyros Caravan and Camping Site

Tenby Bay

CONTENTS

CONTENTS

Vicarious Books

Don't get lost, get your maps from www.Vicarious-Shop.com. Extensive range of road atlases and sheet maps for the UK and Europe all sold at RRP with free UK P&P.

To order, give us a call or visit our website to buy online.

Tel: 0131 2083333   www.Vicarious-Shop.com

Chapel at Mwnt

Port at Parrog

Vicarious Books

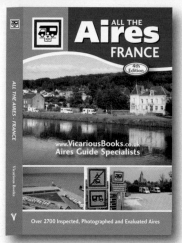

ALL THE Aires FRANCE
4th Edition

ALL THE AIRES - FRANCE

Vicarious Books

www.VicariousBooks.co.uk
Aires Guide Specialists

V

Over 2700 Inspected, Photographed and Evaluated Aires

Motorhomers and campervanners have the privilege of stopping overnight all over Europe at stopovers known as Aires. For more information, visit www.all-the-aires.co.uk.

| MONTRESOR | T | 44 | F6 | N47°09.464' E001°12.100' | 37460 |

Directions: Rue du 8 Mai. Exit village on D10, sp 'Genille'. Turn right, sp 'Toutes Directions'. At roundabout go straight over, sp 'College'. Aire on left, sp 'Tennis'.

Sanitation:

Parking:

35

Flot Bleu Fontaine

Overlooking the château, church and general view of a Village of France that is worth a visit.

Sample France entry with corresponding mapping. Similar mapping for Spain and Portugal and Belgium, Luxembourg and Holland.

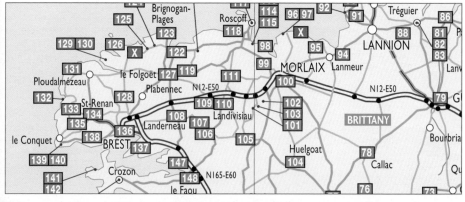

To order, give us a call or visit our website to buy online.

Tel: 0131 2083333   www.Vicarious-Shop.com

Vicarious Books

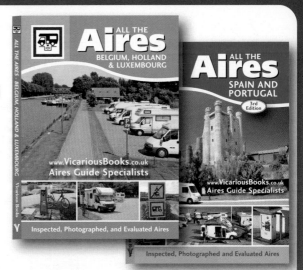

- 2700 Aires for France
- 303 Aires for Spain and Portugal
- 121 Aires for Holland
- 78 Aires for Belgium, plus 10 for Luxembourg
- Extensive LPG listings for every country

Sample Spain and Portugal entry. Entries for Belgium, Luxembourg and Holland follow the same format.

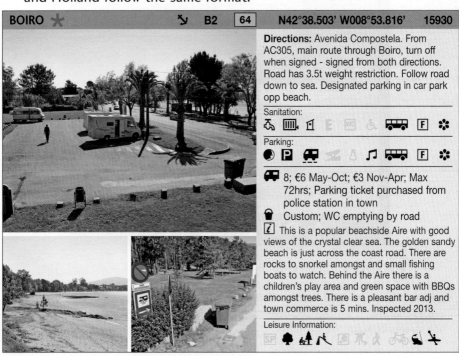

BOIRO ✳   ⚓ **B2** 64   N42°38.503' W008°53.816'   15930

Directions: Avenida Compostela. From AC305, main route through Boiro, turn off when signed - signed from both directions. Road has 3.5t weight restriction. Follow road down to sea. Designated parking in car park opp beach.

Sanitation:

Parking:

🚐 8; €6 May-Oct; €3 Nov-Apr; Max 72hrs; Parking ticket purchased from police station in town

⚓ Custom; WC emptying by road

ℹ️ This is a popular beachside Aire with good views of the crystal clear sea. The golden sandy beach is just across the coast road. There are rocks to snorkel amongst and small fishing boats to watch. Behind the Aire there is a children's play area and green space with BBQs amongst trees. There is a pleasant bar adj and town commerce is 5 mins. Inspected 2013.

Leisure Information:

To order, give us a call or visit our website to buy online.

Tel: 0131 2083333   www.Vicarious-Shop.com

Vicarious Books

- Driving tour suitable for Motorbikes, Cars, Campervans and Motorhomes
- Details car parking, campsites, motorhome stopovers and hotels
- GPS coordinates provided for all sights and accommodation
- Town plans and walking tours for easy navigation on foot

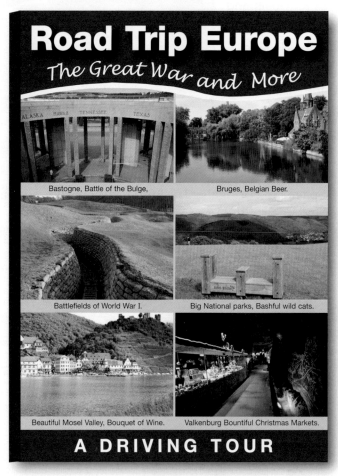

Road Trip Europe
The Great War and More

Bastogne, Battle of the Bulge,

Bruges, Belgian Beer.

Battlefields of World War I.

Big National parks, Bashful wild cats.

Beautiful Mosel Valley, Bouquet of Wine.

Valkenburg Bountiful Christmas Markets.

A DRIVING TOUR

This driving tour encompasses five cities, four countries, and two world wars. The tour visits one of the most beautiful sections of river in Europe, a Roman capital, a national park where wild cats roam free and a town where Christmas decorations are sold all year. It will take you from the highest point in the Netherlands to below the streets of Arras.

To order, give us a call or visit our website to buy online.

Tel: 0131 2083333   www.Vicarious-Shop.com

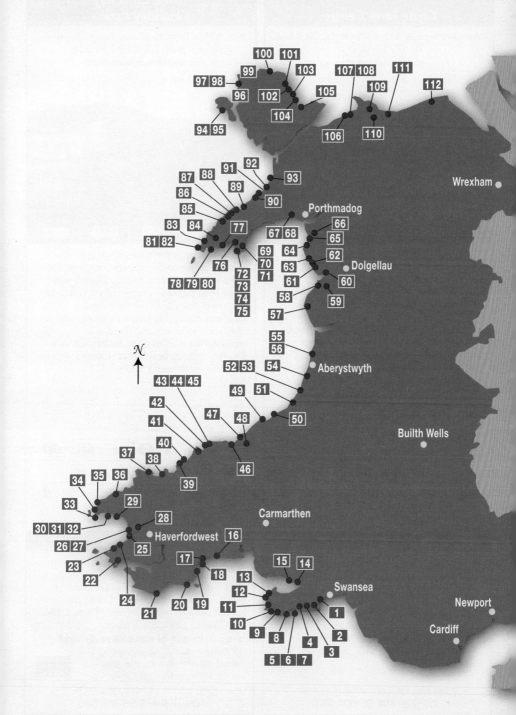

N

Wrexham

Porthmadog

Dolgellau

Aberystwyth

Builth Wells

Carmarthen

Haverfordwest

Swansea

Newport

Cardiff

Clyne Farm Centre

Westport Avenue, Mayals, Swansea, SA3 5AR
Tel: 01792 403333
www.clynefarm.com

This farm based activity centre has camping fields and a woodland camping area where open fires are allowed. Although partly restricted by trees, there are views of Swansea Bay from some pitches. Facilities including toilets, showers, washing machine and dryer are located in a converted barn which also serves as a dry shelter during inclement weather. Booking is essential for activities, which include riding, canoeing, archery, an indoor climbing wall, bush craft and 'the muddiest assault course in the world'. Reception stocks a small selection of basics and includes a coffee shop. Swansea city centre is just 4 miles.

| NA | 1.5 | NP | 30 | 0 AMP | | |

Pub 1 mile. Shop 3 miles.

££££ 🐕 ♦♦ M CL CS ⓘ WiFi

Directions: From Swansea, travel west on A4067 following sp 'South Gower'. Turn right onto B4436 Mayals Road. In 0.5 miles turn right onto Westport Avenue, drive to the top of the hill and turn right again sp 'Clyne Farm Centre'. The centre is at the end of the track with reception on the left of the farmhouse. Use satnav with caution on Gower.

GPS: N51°35.966' W004°00.746'
OS grid: 159 SS 607 908

All year

Three Cliffs Bay Holiday Park

North Hills Farm, Penmaen, Gower, Swansea, SA3 2HB Tel: 01792 371218
www.threecliffsbay.com

Most pitches in the main camping field provide an absolutely superb view over Three Cliffs Bay. This field is mostly sloping with some level pitches. A second field is flat, but the sea is not visible. All facilities are excellent. Reception houses a small shop which stocks basics and there is a supermarket 4 miles away. Nearby Oxwich Bay has a sandy beach that is always popular, especially with young families.

| NA | 5 | NP | 100 | 8 AMP | | |

Pub 1 mile. Slipway 2 miles at Oxwich.

££££ 🐕 ♦♦ M CL CS ⓘ WiFi

Directions: The site is off A4118 between Swansea and Port Eynon. Travelling west, pass the Gower Heritage Centre and in 1 mile turn sharp left off A4118 onto the narrow road sp 'Penmaen' and 'Three Cliffs Bay Touring Site' on the fence. Users of long units may have difficulty negotiating this turn. Follow narrow road to site. Use satnav with caution on Gower.

Cymru
Wales
★★★★

GPS: N51°34.674' W004°06.969'
OS grid: 159 SS 535 886

Easter - October

Nicholaston Farm [3]
Caravan and Camping Site

Penmaen, Gower, Swansea, SA3 2HL
Tel: 01792 371209
www.nicholastonfarm.co.uk

This working farm has three fields providing mostly sloping accommodation. Most pitches on the touring field offer fine south facing views overlooking beautiful Oxwich Bay. The showers and toilets are nicely incorporated into the farm buildings and are well kept. The site has a farm shop, a café and Pick Your Own Fruit in season. The beach is a short walk away and Oxwich is a couple of miles further along the beach.

NA	14	NP	120	10 AMP		
WC					MG	MB

Pub and slipway 2 miles at Oxwich.

£££

Directions: The site is off A4118 between Swansea and Port Eynon. Travelling west, pass through Penmaen and turn left off A4118 clearly sp with a campsite symbol and 'Nicholaston Farm'. Park in the farmyard, reception is in the farm shop/café. Use satnav with caution on Gower.

GPS: N51°34.477' W004°07.991'
OS grid: 159 SS 523 884

March - October

Perriswood [4]
Archery and Falconry Centre CL

Perriswood Farm, Penmaen, Gower,
Swansea, SA3 2HN Tel: 01792 371661
www.perriswood.com

Perriswood Archery and Falconry centre also has a Caravan Club CL. There's a fine view across Oxwich Bay from the camping paddock which is slightly sloping. The toilets are a short walk and are available for all site users. There is a coffee shop/café on site. Book in advance if you want to have a go at archery, airgun shooting or falconry.

NA	0.3	NP	5	6-10 AMP		
WC					MG	MB

Pub and slipway 2 miles.

££

Directions: The site is adjacent to A4118 0.75 miles west of Nicholaston. The Archery and Falconry Centre is well sp from the road and the CL is on the left before the centre car park. Use satnav with caution on Gower.

GPS: N51°34.536' W004°09.293'
OS grid: 159 SS 507 885

March - November

Greenways Holiday Park

Oxwich, South Gower, Swansea, SA3 1LY
Tel: 01792 390220
www.greenwaysleisure.co.uk/camping

This is a well kept 4-star leisure park that accepts tents only and is family oriented with families and couples being preferred. The camping area is spread over several fields, all with outstanding views across Oxwich Bay. The static caravans and onsite bar/clubhouse are all hidden from view from the camping fields. The amenity block has been refurbished. The facilities are excellent and include under floor heating, hot water on demand, washers and dryers. Oxwich is about 0.5 miles downhill from the site and has a small supermarket, café, and hotel with bar and restaurant. Surfing, windsurfing and kayak hire are all available at the beach and there is a slipway for launching small boats.

NA 15   NP 200   0 AMP

WC

Shop, beach and slipway 0.5 miles.

£££

Directions: Turn left off A4118 1.25 miles past Nicholaston sp 'Oxwich'. Go down the steep hill, past the nature reserve and straight on at the crossroads. The site 0.25 miles on the right. Use satnav with caution on Gower.

Cymru Wales

★★★★

GPS: N51°33.307' W004°10.304'
OS grid: 159 SS 495 862

April - September

Oxwich Camping Park

Oxwich, Gower, Swansea, SA3 1LS
Tel: 01792 390777
www.oxwichcampingpark.co.uk

Family oriented and family run, this is a pleasant relaxed site accommodating tents and trailer tents only. The site is situated at the top of a tree lined valley above Oxwich village. From the upper part of the site there is a good view of Oxwich Bay. Some level pitches are available but much of the site is slightly sloping. It is a short walk to Oxwich which has a small supermarket, café, and hotel with bar and restaurant. Surfing, windsurfing and kayak hire are all available at the beach and there is a slipway for launching small boats.

NA 10   NP 180   0 AMP

WC   dryers only

Pub, shop, slipway and beach 0.5 miles.

£££

Directions: Turn off A4118 1.25 miles past Nicholaston sp 'Oxwich'. Go down the steep hill, past the nature reserve and turn right at the crossroads. The site is 0.4 miles on the right. Use satnav with caution on Gower.

GPS: N51°33.562' W004°10.354'
OS grid: 159 SS 494 867

April - September

Eastern Slade Farm

Lundy View, Eastern Slade Farm, Oxwich, Gower, Swansea, SA3 1NA Tel: 01792 391374
www.easternsladecampsite.freeservers.com

There is a fine sea view to Port Eynon Bay from this mainly sloping site which happens to be the oldest registered campsite on Gower. It has not been ravaged by modernisation providing a get away from it all atmosphere where you can enjoy camping as it should be: plenty of fresh air, a water tap and the stars. There are a couple of portable toilets and chemical toilet disposal is available at the farm. The small beach down the road is normally very quiet as there is no car parking. Surfing, windsurfing and kayak hire are available at the beach and there is a slipway for small boats.

| NA | 1 | NP | 20 | 0 AMP | | |
| WC | | | | | MG | MB |

Pub, shop and slipway 1 mile. Beach 0.25 miles.

££££ 🐾 †† M CL CS ⓘ WiFi

Directions: Turn off A4118 1.25 miles past Nicholaston sp 'Oxwich'. Go down the steep hill, past the nature reserve and straight on at the crossroads. In 1 mile enter the camping field via a sharp left turn. If too tight for your unit continue down the hill and turn around at the farmyard on the right. Upon arrival either call at Lundy View (2nd house on the right down the hill) or phone 07970 969814. Use satnav with caution on Gower.

GPS: N51°33.143'W004°10.889'
OS grid: 159 SS 487 859

All year

Newpark Holiday Park

Port Eynon, Gower, Swansea, SA3 1NP
Tel: 01792 390292
www.newparkholidaypark.co.uk

(off peak)

Newpark is a traditional family site comprising static caravans and touring pitches with a separate terraced field for tents. Facilities are clean and well maintained. There are good sea views across Port Eynon Bay from the touring pitches. The small onsite shop stocks day-to-day essentials. You can walk to Port Eynon village without walking on roads. The beach is 0.5 miles downhill.

| NA | 17 | NP | 112 | 10 AMP | | |
| WC | | | | | MG | MB |

Pub, beach and slipway 0.5 miles.

£££ 🐾 †† M CL CS ⓘ WiFi

Directions: The site is adjacent to A4118 just before entering Port Eynon. On entering the site, turn right and follow the road around to reception. Use satnav with caution on Gower.

GPS: N51°32.949' W004°12.955'
OS grid: 159 SS 464 856

April - October

Bank Farm Leisure

Horton, Gower, Swansea, SA3 1LL
Tel: 01792 390228
www.bankfarmleisure.co.uk

Bank Farm is a large and very popular 3-star leisure park with wide sea views across Port Eynon Bay from virtually the entire site. There are extensive camping fields, seasonal pitches, static caravans and holiday accommodation spread out on several levels. The comprehensive facilities include an onsite shop and bar/restaurant, all of which are maintained to a good standard. Access to the beach is at Horton 0.25 miles downhill.

| NA | 75 | NP | 250 | 10 AMP | | |

| WC | | | | | | MG | |

Beach 0.25 miles. Slipway 1 mile.

£££

Directions: The site entrance is off A4118, 0.5 miles north of Port Eynon. Travelling west turn left off A4118 sp 'Horton'. In 100m turn right onto the site road sp with a campsite symbol and 'Bank Farm'. Follow this road all the way around to reception. Using this entrance avoids narrow roads in Horton village. Use satnav with caution on Gower.

Cymru Wales
★★★

GPS: N51°33.369' W004°12.847'
OS grid: 159 SS 471 859

March - November

Pitton Cross Caravan and Camping Park

Rhossili, Gower, Swansea, SA3 1PT
Tel: 01792 390593
www.pittoncross.co.uk

This is a family run campsite with modern facilities that are well kept. From most of the site there is a view of the sea across fields. The pitching areas are nicely laid out and are divided by trees and hedges. The site shop stocks most essentials and has a selection of local produce as well as housing the Gower Kite Centre with a range of stock. Rhossili and the fabulous long sand beach are 1.5 miles away. Various walks are signed from the site. Over 50's can take advantage of reduced rates for weekly bookings out of season.

| NA | 6 | NP | 100 | 10 AMP | | |

| WC | | | | | | MG | |

Pub and beach 1.5 miles.

£££

Directions: The site is adjacent to B4247 1 mile east of Rhossili. From A4118 turn onto B4247 in Scurlage sp with a campsite symbol and 'Pitton Cross'. The site is 2.25 miles on the left. Use satnav with caution on Gower.

GPS: N51°34.065' W004°15.637'
OS grid: 159 SS 434 878

All year

Hillend
Caravan and Camping Park

Hillend, Llangennith, Gower, Swansea,
SA3 1JD Tel: 01792 386204
www.hillendcamping.com

Situated behind the sand dunes in the middle of beautiful Rhossili Bay, some parts of this site offer glimpses of the sea between the dunes. Its location makes it popular with surfers and it is very busy in summer. Two of the four fields are reserved for families and couples only. Facilities are modern and of a high standard. Eddy's Café/Bar serves food and drinks all day and you can enjoy a fine view over the dunes out to sea from inside the café or from its extensive terrace. Advanced bookings are not taken and caravans are not accepted.

| NA 14 | NP 300 | 0 AMP | | |

£££

Directions: Follow B4295 west from Gowerton for 14 miles until you reach Llangennith. Pass the King's Head pub on the right and then turn left at the next crossroads. Follow the narrow road for 0.75 miles to the site. Use satnav with caution on Gower.

GPS: N51°35.643' W004°17.166'
OS grid: 159 SS 417 908

April - October

Llanmadoc
Camping and Caravan Site

Lagadranta Farm, Llanmadoc, Gower, Swansea,
SA3 1DE Tel: 01792 386202
www.gowercampsite.co.uk

This traditional family farm and simple campsite offers good views of Broughton Bay from the slightly sloping fields. This peaceful site provides everything you need for a great family beach holiday because there easy access to the dunes and a large sandy beach. The site accepts families and couples only and operates a 10pm noise curfew.

| NA 12.5 | NP 280 | 10 AMP | | |

£££

Directions: Follow B4295 west from Gowerton for 7.75 miles past Llanrhidian to Oldwalls. Turn right at the Greyhound Inn sp 'Llanmadoc'. Bear left in Llanmadoc sp 'Broughton Beach' and the site is in 0.75 miles at the end of the road. Use satnav with caution on Gower.

GPS: N51°36.933' W004°16.324'
OS grid: 159 SS 427 931

May - October

Orchard Park Farm *CL* [13]

Llanmadoc, Gower, Swansea, SA3 1DE
Tel: 01792 386670

This slightly sloping Caravan Club *CL* provides a good view across fields to Broughton Bay. The site is just outside Llanmadoc village which has a pub and its own community run shop and post office. The Wales Coast Path runs along the dunes nearby leading onto a huge stretch of National Trust marshland northeast of the site.

| NA | 0.5 | NP | 5 | 10 AMP | | |

Pub, shop and beach 0.5 miles.

££££ 🐕 †† M *CL* CS ⓘ WiFi

Directions: Follow B4295 west from Gowerton for 7.75 miles past Llanrhidian to Oldwalls. Turn right at the Greyhound Inn sp 'Llanmadoc'. Bear left in Llanmadoc sp 'Broughton Beach' and the site is in 0.5 miles just outside the village. Just drive in and pitch, the owner will call. Use satnav with caution on Gower.

GPS: N51°37.104' W004°15.870'
OS grid: 159 SS 433 934

March - October

Gateway Holiday Park [14]

Millennium Coast, Bynea, Llanelli, SA14 9SN Tel: 01554 771202
www.caravanparkgower.co.uk

Occupying 35 acres, most touring pitches on this large holiday park offer views across the Loughor Estuary towards the Gower. The site provides family oriented holidays as well as seasonal pitches. Touring pitches are on both grass and hardstanding and a less formal field accommodates tents in summer. The onsite clubhouse and bars provide plenty of entertainment and there is also an indoor heated swimming pool, games room, play centre, a fishing lake and a slipway.

| NA | 35 | NP | 200 | 16 AMP | | |

£££ 🐕 †† M *CL* CS ⓘ WiFi

Directions: The site is well sp off A484 2.5 miles east of Llanelli.

GPS: N51°39.849' W004°06.229'
OS grid: 159 SS 545 982

All year

Caemawr Caravanning CS 〔15〕

Caemawr Farm, Furnace, Llanelli, SA15 4NU
Tel: 07711 274687
www.caemawrcaravanning.co.uk

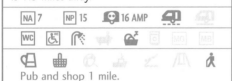

From this 7 acre field there are views across the Loughor Estuary and Llanrhidian Sands to the Gower Peninsula. A gravel road along the top of the field also provides 20 hardstandings for parking and pitching. 5 touring pitches have electric hook-up. There is plenty of space for tents and rallies can be accommodated. Toilets and showers are available at the farm. The Celtic Trail cycleway and the Millennium Coast Park are both nearby offering 20km of traffic free cycling. The Wales Coast Path can be joined by following the footpath that runs past the site. Llanelli, the largest town in Carmarthenshire, is 1.5 miles away.

NA 7	NP 15	🗝 16 AMP		
WC						

Pub and shop 1 mile.

££££ 🐕 ♦♦ M CL CS ⓘ WiFi

Directions: From Llanelli, head north on B4309 New Road sp 'Furnace'. Go straight over roundabout, then turn right into Pentrepoeth Road. At the end of the road, turn left. Caemawr is the 1st farm on the left, 0.25 miles up the hill.

GPS: N51°41.843' W004°09.498'
OS grid: 159 SN 509 020

All year

Meadow House Holiday Park 〔16〕

Summerhill, Amroth, SA67 8NS
Tel: 01834 812438
www.celticholidayparks.com

Views over hedges to Carmarthen Bay can be enjoyed from the motorhome and caravan touring field. Pitches are a mix of grass and hardstandings, all are serviced with hook-ups and there is a separate field for tents. There are six other areas accommodating static caravans. Onsite facilities include a heated indoor swimming pool and a bar with entertainment on Saturdays during high season. From site there is direct access to the Wales Coast Path and it's less than 1 mile to the beaches at Amroth or Wiseman's Bridge.

NA 16	NP 70	🗝 10 AMP		
WC						

Shop and beach 0.75 miles.

£££ 🐕 ♦♦ M CL CS ⓘ WiFi

Directions: Take A477 south from St Clears towards Pembroke. Turn left sp 'Amroth' and 'Wisemans Bridge' with a campsite symbol. In 1 mile turn left sp 'Summerhill', 'Amroth' and 'Wiseman's Bridge'. Follow road for 0.5 miles and the park entrance is on the left.

GPS: N51°43.926' W004°40.521'
OS grid: 158 SN 153 070

March - October

Trevayne Farm Caravan and Camping Park 17

Monkstone, Saundersfoot, Pembrokeshire,
SA69 9DL Tel: 01834 813402
www.trevaynefarm.co.uk

This is a popular family site on a working farm. The pitches are spread over several fields and it is necessary to request a pitch with a sea view when booking. The site facilities are very good. There is private access to the beach at Monkstone Bay, 10 mins walk down a cliff path with steps all the way. Bass and mackerel fishing are reportedly good at high tide here. At low tide a large sandy beach is created providing a lovely alternative to the busier beaches at Saundersfoot and Tenby, which have all the attractions you would expect of popular seaside resorts.

| NA 21 | NP 120 | 10-16 AMP |

| WC | | | | | MG | MB |

Pub 1 mile at New Hedges. Slipway 1.5 miles at Saundersfoot. Note: MB down a manhole.

£££

Directions: From the A478/A477 roundabout junction, take A478 south sp 'Tenby'. At the New Hedges bypass roundabout, turn left onto B4316 then take the 1st right sp 'New Hedges'. Turn immediately left sp 'Trevayne'. The site is in 0.75 miles at the end of the road.

GPS: N51°41.776' W004°41.467'
OS grid: 158 SN 141 032

April - October

Windmills Caravan Park 18

Slippery Back, Tenby, Pembrokeshire,
SA70 8TJ
Tel: 01834 842200

Windmills is a quiet, select site with beautifully kept, closely mown grass. The facilities, although not new, are well kept and clean. There are good sea views over to Tenby and Caldy Island. A footpath at the site entrance takes you 0.75 miles downhill to North Beach and Tenby. The traditional seaside town of Tenby has all the attractions you would expect of a popular seaside resort and offers cafés and restaurants appealing to all tastes and budgets. The Wales Coast Path passes nearby.

| NA 4 | NP 15 | 10 AMP |

| WC | | | | | MG | MB |

Pub and shop 0.5 miles at New Hedges. Beach 0.75 miles. Slipway 2 miles at Saundersfoot.

£££

Directions: Heading south on A478 towards Tenby, drive through New Hedges and turn 3rd left into Slippery Back sp with a campsite symbol and 'Windmills Caravan Park'.

GPS: N51°41.056' W004°42.523'
OS grid: 158 SN 129 018

April - October

Meadow Farm

Northcliffe, Tenby, SA70 8AU
Tel: 01834 844829
www.meadowfarmtenby.co.uk

This simple, get away from it all farm site offers a fine view across the town and the bay from the partly sloping grass main field. Facilities are old and basic, but clean. The traditional seaside town of Tenby is only 0.5 miles' walk downhill and has all the attractions you would expect of a popular resort. There are cafés and restaurants appealing to all tastes and budgets. You can follow the Wales Coast Path from site to Tenby harbour and St Catherine's Island which is accessible for 6 hours during low tide. Entrance fees are £2 for adults and £1 for children. Tours of the Napoleonic fort should commence during 2014 subject to safety works being completed.

| NA 1.5 | NP 38 | 16 AMP | | |

Pub, shop, beach and slipway 0.5 miles.

£££

Directions: From A478 seafront road in Tenby, turn into The Croft by the Cliffe-Norton Hotel sp 'Fourcroft Hotel' and 'Park Hotel'. Continue for 0.5 miles keeping North Beach on your right, then turn left up the narrow lane sp 'Meadow Farm'. The farm entrance is the 2nd gate on the left.

GPS: N51°40.896' W004°42.098'
OS grid: 158 SN 133 015

March - October

Wynd Hill Farm

Manorbier, Tenby, Pembrokeshire, SA70 7SL
Tel: 01834 871472

This simple site provides sea views across fields in two directions. 4 small, concrete hardstandings break up the flat grass. Facilities are not new, but are clean. Manorbier village is 0.75 miles away and has a local shop and pub as well as a Norman castle. Continue a further 0.25 miles to the Blue Flag beach at Manorbier Bay.

| NA 2 | NP 14 | 16 AMP | | |

Pub, shop and beach 0.5 miles.

££

Directions: The site is adjacent to A4139 Tenby-Pembroke road, 0.5 miles west of the village of Lydstep. From Tenby follow A4139 west for 4.5 miles to the site on the left. Turn left into the entrance, then immediately left again into the walled area. Call at the house upon arrival.

GPS: N51°39.070' W004°46.990'
OS grid: 158 SS 075 983

All year

Trefalen Farm

Bosherston, Pembroke, Pembrokeshire,
SA71 5DR
Tel: 01646 661643

This is a 'back to basics', informal farm site with two camping fields that also provide grazing for sheep when the site is unoccupied. The sheep are the only lawn mowers so the grass may be long. One field is mainly flat and used for caravans and motorhomes, the other is partly sloping and used mainly for tents and small campervans. The site facilities, although basic, are well kept and clean. It's a short walk to the unspoilt sandy beach of Broadhaven and the site is adjacent to the Wales Coast Path and the National Trust's Stackpole Estate.

| NA | 20 | NP | 90 | 0 AMP | | |

| WC | | | | | | MC | MB |

Pub 0.75 miles. Shop 5 miles. Slipway 3 miles.

££££ 🐕 ♂♀ M CL CS ⓘ WiFi

Directions: Take B4319 south from Pembroke following sp 'Bosherston'. Follow road through Bosherston and then turn left sp 'Broad Haven'. The site is in 1 mile just before the car park at the end of the road. Call at the white farmhouse. Users of caravans or large motorhomes must telephone in advance as there is alternate access for large vehicles.

GPS: N51°36.443' W004°55.635'
OS grid: 158 SR 974 939

All Year

Windmill Farm *CS*

Dale, Haverfordwest, Pembrokeshire,
SA62 3QX
Tel: 01646 636428

This site has a fine sea view across Milford Haven. The field is sloping, but there are terraced pitches for motorhomes and caravans. The attractive, well kept toilet and shower facilities are incorporated into the old farm buildings and there is also a book swap shelf. The Wales Coast Path passes by and around Milford Haven bay which becomes a large area of exposed beach at low tide.

| NA | 1 | NP | 15 | | | |

| WC | | | | | | MC | MB |

Pub, shop (seasonal), beach and slipway all less than 1 mile at Dale.

££££ 🐕 ♂♀ M CL *CS* ⓘ WiFi

Directions: The site is adjacent to B4327 1 mile north of Dale. The farm is sp on the right shortly after the beach parking area on the left.

GPS: N51°42.854' W005°10.378'
OS grid: 157 SM 809 065

March - October

Mill Haven Place CS

Middle Broadmoor Farm, Talbenny,
Haverfordwest, SA62 3XD Tel: 01437 781633
www.millhavenplace.co.uk

Located 1 mile from the little cove at Mill Haven, this family run CS has distant views of the sea through trees. There is a 1 acre camping field as well as fully furnished yurts and a holiday cottage. Each pitch has a picnic table, a BBQ and a fire pit (wood is available). The shower/toilet block is a few metres from the field with a family shower room with toilet and a further individual toilet and shower. A fridge and freezer are also available for use. This is chilled out camping at its best!

NA 4   NP 5   0 AMP

WC

Pub 1.5 miles at Little Haven. Shop 2 miles at Broad Haven. Beach 1 mile at Mill Haven.

£££ M CL CS

Directions: Take B4327 southwest from Haverfordwest towards Dale. After 6.5 miles turn right by Hasguard Cross Caravan Park sp 'Little Haven'. Follow road through Talbenny and go straight on at crossroads. The site is 0.6 miles further on the right.

GPS: N51°45.820' W005°08.867'
OS grid: 157 SM 829 119

Easter - September

Howelston Holiday Park

Howelston, Little Haven, Pembrokeshire,
SA62 3UU Tel: 01437 781818
www.sunnyvaleholidaypark.com/howelstonholidaypark.html

This small holiday park is well laid out and accommodates about 60 statics. The six touring pitches are along the top edge of central grass area and benefit from good views over St Brides Bay. The site is fairly quiet and has no clubhouse, but Howelston residents may use the clubhouse and indoor pool at the sister site near Saundersfoot. Little Haven is just over 0.5 miles away by road and a little further via the Wales Coast Path which you can access directly from site.

NA 0.5   NP 6   16 AMP

WC

Pub, beach and slipway 0.5 miles at Little Haven. Shop 1 mile at Broad Haven.

£££ M CL CS

Directions: To avoid narrow lanes in Little Haven, take B4327 southwest from Haverfordwest towards Dale. After 6.5 miles turn right by Hasguard Cross Caravan Park sp 'Little Haven'. Then turn right again sp with a campsite symbol and 'Little Haven'. The site is on the left in just over 0.5 miles.

GPS: N51°45.942' W005°06.946'
OS grid: 157 SM 851 120

March - December

Bower Farm CS

Little Haven, Haverfordwest, Pembrokeshire,
SA62 3TY Tel: 01437 781554
www.bowerfarm.co.uk

This site has a great view across Broad Haven to St Brides Bay. The large field is mainly sloping with a fairly level area at the top for caravans and motorhomes. Shower and toilet facilities are in a wooden shed, but quite acceptable. A 0.5 miles' walk downhill takes you to Broad Haven where you can join the Wales Coast Path and follow it up or down the coast.

| NA 2 | NP 5 | 16 AMP | | |

| WC | | | | | | | |

Pub, shop, beach and slipway 0.5 miles at Broad Haven.

£££ 🐕 M CL CS (i) WiFi

Directions: From Haverfordwest, take B4341 west towards Broad Haven for 4.5 miles, then bear left onto a single-track road sp 'Little Haven'. The site is on the right in 0.4 miles.

GPS: N51°46.697' W005°05.331'
OS grid: 157 SM 870 134

All year

Druidston Home Farm CS

Haverfordwest, Pembrokeshire, SA62 3NE
Tel: 01437 781557
www.druidstonhomefarm.co.uk

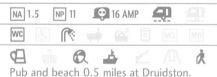

The CS and separate tent field both enjoy fine sea views of St Brides Bay. Non-members can camp in the tent field which is sloping, but members with caravans and motorhomes can find some level areas on the CS field. Toilet and shower facilities are located in a wooden shed adjacent to the farmhouse and were very clean and well kept. There is a bridleway 300m from the site which leads to the beach at Druidston Haven and connects to the Wales Coast Path.

| NA 1.5 | NP 11 | 16 AMP | | |

| WC | | | | | | | |

Pub and beach 0.5 miles at Druidston. Slipway 2 miles at Nolten Haven.

££££ 🐕 M CL CS (i) WiFi
except tents

Directions: From Haverfordwest take A487 west for 4.5 miles to Simpsons Cross. Turn left sp 'Nolton Haven'. Go straight across the next crossroads, then turn right at red phone box in 0.75 miles. The site is on the left in 0.25 miles.

GPS: N51°48.411' W005°05.298'
OS grid: 157 SM 872 165

April - September

Nolton Cross Caravan Park

Nolton Cross, Haverfordwest, Pembrokeshire,
SA62 3NP Tel: 01437 710701
www.noltoncross-holidays.co.uk

Over the banks surrounding this park there is a distant view of St Brides Bay. The relatively quiet site houses 30 statics and has a separate area with 15 touring pitches, each with electric. There is a small, very basic facilities block on the touring field, but a larger and better quality block is near the park entrance. A small lake adjacent to the park is stocked for coarse fishing and equipment is available for hire.

| NA | 1.5 | NP | 15 | ☠ 16 AMP | |

| WC | | | | | |

Pub, shop and slipway 1.5 miles at Nolton Haven.

£££ 🐕 †† M CL CS ⓘ WiFi

Directions: From Haverfordwest, take A487 west for 4.5 miles to Simpsons Cross. Turn left sp 'Nolton Haven'. Turn left again at the next crossroads and the site entrance is 100m on the right.

Cymru Wales
★★★

GPS: N51°48.957' W005°04.759'
OS grid: 157 SM 878 175

March - November

Shortlands Farm *CL*

Druidston, Haverfordwest, Pembrokeshire,
SA62 3NE Tel: 01437 781234
www.shortlandsfarm.co.uk

This small dairy farm enjoys a wide view of St Brides Bay from its Caravan Club *CL* and its camping field which is open to non-members. Each pitch at the *CL* has electric hook-up. Shower and toilet facilities are available to all campers and are adjacent to the farmhouse close to the camping field. The site is situated at the end of a lane which continues as a bridleway for 0.5 miles towards the beach at Druidston Haven and the Wales Coast Path.

| NA | 1 | NP | 15 | ☠ 6 AMP | |

| WC | | | | | |

Pub and beach 0.5 miles at Druidston. Slipway 2 miles at Nolten Haven.

££ 🐕 †† M *CL* CS ⓘ WiFi
except tents

Directions: From Haverfordwest, take A487 west for 4.5 miles to Simpsons Cross. Turn left sp 'Nolton Haven'. Go straight across the next crossroads, then turn right at the red phone box in 0.75 miles. Follow this road to the site at the end of the lane (the road gets very bumpy).

GPS: N51°48.463' W005°05.701'
OS grid: 157 SM 867 166

All year

Nine Wells
Caravan and Camping Park `29`

Nine Wells, Nr St David's, Pembrokeshire,
SA62 6UH Tel: 01437 721809
www.ninewellscamping.com

You can enjoy a view of St Brides Bay from the top of this laidback site. The field is sloping, but a few level spots are available. The refurbished shower block and toilets are well kept and supply free hot water for showers and washing up. Walk for 5 mins down a footpath from site to the Wales Coast Path and a small pebbly cove overlooked by Porth-y-Rhaw, an Iron Age fort. St David's is 2 miles away. Attractions include the cathedral and a medieval bishop's palace.

| NA 4 | NP 60 | 10 AMP | | |

| WC | | | | | | MG | MB |

Pub, shop and beach 1.5 miles at Solva.

£££

Directions: The site is adjacent to A487, 2.25 miles east of St David's. Turn off in Nine Wells sp for the campsite. The site entrance is 180m on the right. Choose your pitch and the site owner will call and collect payment.

GPS: N51°52.704' W005°12.982'
OS grid: 157 SM 787 248

All year

Caerfai Bay
Caravan and Tent Park `30`

St David's, Haverfordwest, Pembrokeshire,
SA62 6QT Tel: 01437 720274
www.caerfaibay.co.uk

This well equipped site is popular with families and virtually every pitch has an almost 180° sea view across St Brides Bay. Facilities are excellent and spotlessly clean. The site is right on the Coast Path and it is a short walk down to beautiful Caerfai Bay beach. The amenities of St David's are just a 10 mins walk away. If bringing a dog, please check with the site before booking.

| NA 10 | NP 120 | 10 AMP | | |

| WC | | | | | | MG | MB |

Pub 0.75 miles at St David's. Shop and beach 180m.

£££

Directions: Head east on A487 out of St David's and turn right onto Caerfai Road sp 'Caerfai'. The site is on the right at the end of the road just before the car park.

Cymru
Wales

GPS: N51°52.376' W005°15.419'
OS grid: 157 SM 759 244

March - November

Glan-y-Mor Campsite

Caerfai Road, St David's, Pembrokeshire,
SA62 6QT Tel: 01437 721788
www.glan-y-mor.co.uk

The site is divided into three small, flat fields, all with views to the sea over hedges. Toilet and shower facilities are not new but are perfectly clean and a fridge freezer is available for campers' use. Caerfai Bay and its beautiful sandy beach are only 0.25 miles away and the centre of St David's is just 0.75 miles. There's also a small organic farm shop along the road to the beach. From the beach you can walk along the Wales Coast Path in either direction.

| NA | 2.5 | NP | | 10 AMP | | |

| WC | | | | | | |

Pub and shop 0.75 miles at St David's.

£££

Directions: From Haverfordwest, turn left off A487 at the edge of St David's into Caerfai Road sp 'Caerfai' and 'P' for parking. The site is on the left in 0.4 miles.

GPS: N51°52.540' W005°15.601'
OS grid: 157 SM 757 247

April - September

Caerfai Farm Campsite

Caerfai Road, St David's, Pembrokeshire,
SA62 6QT Tel: 01437 720548
www.caerfai.co.uk

The campsite occupies three large fields on a working organic farm situated right above pretty Caerfai Bay with stunning views right across St Brides Bay. Pitches are allocated around the edges of the fields giving a nice open feel to the site. Sustainable farming and renewable energy are primary considerations here and solar, geo-thermal, bio-gas and wind power are all used. During the summer, the farm shop sells organic vegetables, general groceries and award-winning Caerfai Organic Cheeses, which are hand made on the farm.

| NA | 5 | NP | 63 | 10 AMP | | |

| WC | | | | | | |

Pub 0.75 miles at St David's. Beach 140m.

££££

Directions: From Haverfordwest, turn left off A487 at the edge of St David's into Caerfai Road sp 'Caerfai' and 'P' for parking. The site is on the left in 0.5 miles. Stop in at the farm shop just before the site entrance to book in.

Cymru
Wales

GPS: N51°52.404' W005°15.426'
OS grid: 157 SM 759 244

Whitsun - September

Porthclais Farm Campsite

St David's, Pembrokeshire, SA62 6RR
Tel: 01437 720619 or 07970 439310
www.porthclais-farm-campsite.co.uk

This farm-based site is set on a promontory adjacent to the small inlet of Porthclais Harbour with far reaching sea views. The 5 acre touring field is flat but is only licensed for 12 units, so booking is advised. The 24 acres of tent fields are partly sloping. Toilet and shower facilities are good including an additional block available during busy periods. The nearest beach is at Caerfai Bay and the Blue Flag surfing beach at Whitesands is 3 miles away. From the site there is direct access to the Wales Coast Path and down to the harbour.

NA	29	NP	112	0 AMP		
WC					MG	MB

Pub and shop 1 mile at St David's.

£££ M CL CS WiFi

Directions: From St David's city centre follow sp 'Porth Clais' and 'St Justinian' west onto Goat Street, then Catherine Street. The site entrance is on the left in 0.75 miles from the centre of St David's.

GPS: N51°52.276' W005°16.728'
OS grid: 157 SM 744 243

Easter - October

Rhosson Ganol Farm

St David's, Pembrokeshire,
SA62 6PY
Tel: 01437 720361

This basic site is spread over two fields in an idyllic, isolated location with far reaching views across to Ramsey Island. This is a popular, informal site, with some families returning year after year. Shower and toilet facilities are adjacent to the farmhouse across the road and, whilst not new, they are more than adequate and were newly painted and perfectly clean when we visited.

NA	3.5	NP	25	0 AMP		
WC					MG	MB

Pub and shop 1.5 miles at St David's.
Slipway 2 miles at Porthclais.

££££ M CL CS WiFi

Directions: From St David's city centre follow sp 'Porth Clais' and 'St Justinian' west onto Goat Street, then Catherine Street. Then turn sharp right sp 'St Justinian', then sharp left. Follow road for 1.5 miles, pass the owner's farmhouse on the right and the campsite entrance is 90m on the left.

GPS: N51°52.759' W005°18.180'
OS grid: 157 SM 727 252

Easter - October

Whitesands Camping 35

Tan-y-Bryn, Whitesands, St David's,
Pembrokeshire, SA62 6PS Tel: 01437 721472
www.whitesandscamping.co.uk

Photo courtesy of campsite owner

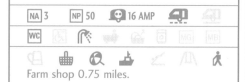

This site may be basic, but it is very well
located right next to the Blue Flag
Whitesands Beach which is popular with
surfers at all times of year. The site occupies
three sloping fields, but some level places are
available on the narrow field nearest the
road. Toilet and shower facilities are old and
basic, but there are public toilets next to the
beach car park which also has a shop/café
open every day during the summer. There is
also a farm shop 0.75 miles away. A surf
school offers lessons and equipment hire
from the beach.

NA 3	NP 50	🙂 16 AMP		
WC				

Farm shop 0.75 miles.

££££ 🐕 ♿ M CL CS ⓘ WiFi

Directions: Follow A487 north out of St
David's, then turn left onto B4583 sp with a
campsite symbol and 'Whitesands'. Turn left
in 0.25 miles to stay on B4583 sp
'Whitesands'. The site is on the right in 1.6
miles, immediately after a small static park
and before the beach car park. Check at the
beach car park kiosk for pitching
information.

GPS: N51°53.855' W005°17.520'
OS grid: 157 SM 735 272

March - October

St David's Camping 36 and Caravanning Club Site

Dwr Cwmwdig Berea, St David's, Haverfordwest,
Pembrokeshire, SA62 6DW Tel: 01348 831376
www.campingandcaravanningclub.co.uk

This mostly sloping hillside site is spread
over two fields with good sea views from the
top field. The toilet and shower facilities are
spotlessly clean, but are not up to the
standard normally found at Camping and
Caravanning Club sites. We understand that
the site is due to be upgraded and expanded
shortly. The beach at Abereiddy is 1 mile
away via a footpath and St David's and all its
conveniences are 5 miles away.

NA 2.5	NP 40	🙂 16 AMP		
WC				

Pub 1 mile at Croes Goch. Shop basics onsite
otherwise 5 miles at St David's. Beach 1 mile.

£££ 🐕 ♿ M CL CS ⓘ WiFi

Directions: 7.1 miles north of St David's
turn west off A487 at Croes-goch sp with a
campsite symbol and 'Abereiddy'. After 1
mile turn right sp with a campsite symbol
and 'Abereiddy'. Turn left at the next
crossroads, then turn left again and the site
is 0.25 miles on the left.

GPS: N51°55.795' W005°11.514'
OS grid: 157 SM 807 305

April - September

The Seaview Hotel `37`

Fishguard, Pembrokeshire, SA65 9PL
Tel: 01348 874282
www.fishguardhotel.co.uk

This is a Practical Motorhome Nightstop site, certificated by The Motor Caravanners Club for five motorhomes. Parking is in the hotel car park which has a view of Fishguard Harbour. There are no facilities but the hotel toilets may be used when open. A one night stay is free, but buying a drink or two, or a meal, is appreciated. Upon arrival call at the hotel reception to let them know you are staying.

| NA | NP 5 | 0 AMP | | |

| WC | | | | | | MG | MB |

Shop 0.5 miles.

FREE

Directions: The hotel is adjacent to A40 heading from Fishguard towards the port.

GPS: N51°59.951' W004°59.316'
OS grid: 157 SM 949 376

All year

Fishguard Bay `38`
Caravan and Camping Park

Garn Gelli, Fishguard, Pembrokeshire, SA65 9ET
Tel: 01348 811415
www.fishguardbay.com

(max 8m)

This terraced site is on a headland high above Fishguard Bay. Most pitches are level or slightly sloping and enjoy a great sea view over the bay. The site accommodates mainly static caravans but is attractively laid out with separate areas for touring pitches. The whole site is tidy and well kept and there is a lounge and games room available as well as a small kitchen with microwave cookers and a well equipped launderette.

| NA 3 | NP 50 | 10 AMP | | |

| WC | | | | | | MG | MB |

Pub, shop and slipway 3 miles at Fishguard. Beach 1.5 miles.

£££

Directions: Turn off A487 1.5 miles east of Fishguard onto the no through road sp for the campsite. The site is in 0.75 miles at the end of this narrow road.

Cymru Wales
★★★★

GPS: N52°00.308' W004°56.337'
OS grid: 145 SM 984 382

March - January

Tycanol Farm

Newport, Pembrokeshire, SA42 0ST
Tel: 01239 820264

Situated on a working farm, this relaxed site extends over three fields and has excellent views over Newport Bay. Some of the site is sloping but level pitches are available. Toilet and shower facilities are a little rustic. There is a large open-sided shelter equipped with old chairs and a wood burner which provides a great focus for evening get-togethers. For visitors who don't want to camp, a large room over a barn has been converted into accommodation and equipped with a motley collection of furniture from the 1950's and earlier!

| NA 3 | NP 30 | 10 AMP | | |

| WC | | | | | |

Pub and shop 1 mile at Newport.

£££

Directions: Turn off A487 1 mile west of Newport onto the farm track sp for the campsite. The site is in 0.5 miles at the end of the bumpy track.

GPS: N52°01.150' W004°51.161'
OS grid: 145 SN 043 394

All year

Morawelon
Camping and Caravanning *CS*

Parrog, Newport, Pembrokeshire, SA42 0RW
Tel: 01239 820565
www.campsite-pembrokeshire.co.uk

This CS also has two fields for non-member tents. The site is sloping but this enables good views over Newport Sands or Newport Bay from most pitches. The site is in an attractive location behind the Morawelon restaurant and across the road from the old port of Parrog. There are still some original buildings in the port, one of which houses the local boat club. The site is very popular with boating and water sports enthusiasts.

| NA 5.5 | NP 5 | 16 AMP | | |

| WC | | | | | |

Onsite shop sells basics. Pub and larger shops 0.5 miles in Newport.

£££

Directions: From A487 in Newport, turn onto Parrog Road sp with the campsite symbol and 'Parrog'. Follow the road for 0.4 miles to the end and the site entrance is just past the restaurant. Reception is through the back door of the restaurant.

GPS: N52°01.234' W004°50.497'
OS grid: 145 SN 051 396

March - October

Cardigan Camping and Caravan Site 41

Fishguard Road, Cardigan, SA43 3DR
Tel: 01239 612772
www.cardigancaravansite.co.uk

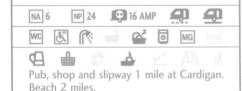

Opened in 2012, this site is set on a large flat field with a limited and distant view of the sea from some pitches. All pitches are hardstanding and there is an excellent facilities block incorporating toilets, showers and a kitchen equipped with washing machine, dryer, fridge freezer and microwave. The owners believe in sustainability and have invested in solar panels for electricity generation and rainwater harvesting for toilet flushing. A borehole provides water for the showers.

| NA 6 | NP 24 | 🛢 16 AMP | | |

| WC | 🦽 | 🚿 | | 📷 | MG | MB |

Pub, shop and slipway 1 mile at Cardigan. Beach 2 miles.

£££ 🐕 †† M CL CS ⓘ WiFi

Directions: Take A487 southwest from Cardigan. Turn right 2 miles before Fishguard onto the farm track sp for the campsite. The site entrance is on the left in 0.7 miles.

Cymru Wales
★★★

GPS: N52°03.990' W004°39.962'
OS grid: 145 SN 174 442

March - January

Nant-y-Croi Farm CS 42

Ferwig, Cardigan, Ceredigion, SA43 1PU
Tel: 01239 614024
www.cardiganbayfarmholidays.co.uk

The large camping field is mainly sloping, but has a level area at the top which enjoys an almost 180° view across Cardigan Bay. Facilities are housed in three modular buildings which are old, but are kept clean. Washing machines and a fridge freezer are available for use at the farmyard. The site is family-friendly and children can help with feeding the animals and walking the farm dogs. You can walk across farmland to join the Wales Coast Path at a rocky cove or take a footpath for 1 mile to the beautiful little National Trust beach at Mwnt where there is a seasonal refreshment kiosk.

| NA 10 | NP 40 | 🛢 16 AMP | | |

| WC | | 🚿 | | 📷 | MO | MB |

Pub and slipway 2 miles at Gwbert. Shop 4 miles at Cardigan.

£££ 🐕 †† M CL CS ⓘ WiFi

Directions: Take B4548 northeast from Cardigan sp 'Gwbert'. At the edge of town turn right sp 'Ferwig' and 'Mwnt'. Follow this road for 2 miles, then turn left at the T-junction. Follow this road through Ferwig. At the edge of the village bear right into a no through road. The site entrance is in 1 mile.

GPS: N52°07.600' W004°39.502'
OS grid: 145 SN 181 509

Easter - October

Ty Gwyn
Caravan and Camping Park

Mwnt, Cardigan, Ceredigion, SA43 1QH
Tel: 01239 614518
www.campingatmwnt.co.uk

There are superb views out over Cardigan Bay from this campsite that is part of a family run farm. The site is spread over several fields which are partly sloping, but most campers should be able to find a level place to pitch. A new toilet and shower block was opened in 2013. Electric hook-ups are limited and must be booked in advance. A 0.25 miles' walk leads to the beautiful little National Trust beach at Mwnt where there is a seasonal refreshment kiosk.

| NA 6 | NP 25 | 🕷 10 AMP | |

Pub 4 miles at Gwbert. Shop 1.25 miles at Blaenwaun Campsite 45 or 5 miles at Cardigan. Beach 0.25 miles.

££ 🐕 M CL

Directions: Take B4548 northeast from Cardigan sp 'Gwbert'. At the edge of town turn right sp 'Ferwig' and 'Mwnt'. Follow this road for 2 miles, then turn right at the T-junction sp 'Mwnt'. Take the 1st left in 50m. Turn left in 0.8 miles sp 'Mwnt'. Drive towards the sea for 0.7 miles. Pass the beach car park and the site is at the end of the road.

GPS: N52°08.170' W004°38.116'
OS grid: 145 SN 198 519

March - October

Ffynnon Grog CL

Mwnt, Cardigan, Ceredigion, SA43 1QH
Tel: 01239 621412

This site is set on a sloping field with fine views over Cardigan Bay. There is fairly level pitching for caravans at the top of the field and long motorhomes may park just inside the gate. Just 0.5 miles away is the beautiful little National Trust beach at Mwnt where there is a seasonal refreshment kiosk.

| NA 12 | NP 5 | 0 AMP | |

Pub 3 miles at Gwbert. Shop 0.25 miles at Blaenwaun Campsite 45 or 4 miles at Cardigan. Beach 0.25 miles.

£££ 🐕 M CL

Directions: Take B4548 northeast from Cardigan sp 'Gwbert'. At the edge of town turn right sp 'Ferwig' and 'Mwnt'. Follow this road for 2 miles, then turn right at the T-junction sp 'Mwnt'. Take the 1st left in 50m. Turn left in 0.8 miles sp 'Mwnt'. Drive towards the sea for 0.1 miles, then turn right into the site.

GPS: N52°07.780' W004°37.977'
OS grid: 145 SN 199 512

Easter - October

Blaenwaun Caravan Park

Mwnt, Cardigan, Ceredigion, SA43 1QF
Tel: 01239 613456
www.blaenwaunfarm.com

This spacious, gently sloping site occupies a large field. Static caravans line the bottom edge and the centrally located touring pitches overlook them and take in panoramic views of Cardigan Bay. The reception, shop and facilities are in attractive log cabin style buildings. Showers, toilets and the utility room are all modern and the utility room houses sinks, washers, dryers, ironing board and iron, a fridge, coffee and cold drinks machines and a microwave. The beautiful, little National Trust beach at Mwnt is 0.75 miles' walk down a footpath. Campers wanting to bring dogs must check with the site in advance.

NA 7	NP 30	10 AMP		

Pub 3.5 miles at Gwbert. Beach 0.75 miles.

£££ 🐕 ⅲ M CL CS ① WiFi

Directions: Take B4548 northeast from Cardigan sp 'Gwbert'. At the edge of town turn right sp 'Ferwig' and 'Mwnt'. Follow this road for 2 miles, then turn right at the T-junction sp for the caravan park. Take the 1st left in 50m and the site is on the left in 1.1 miles.

Cymru Wales
★★★★

GPS: N52°07.828' W004°37.578'
OS grid: 145 SN 204 513

Easter - October

Dolgelynen Caravan Park

Aberporth, Cardigan, Ceredigion, SA43 2HS
Tel: 01239 811095

The site is just 1 mile out of Aberporth and accommodates both static caravans and touring pitches. The partly sloping touring field is separate from the statics and enjoys a good view over the little town out to Cardigan Bay. Toilets, showers and laundry facilities are housed in an old-style block. Aberporth has a Blue Flag beach with a dog-friendly area.

NA 2.5	NP 42	16 AMP		

Pub, shop, beach and slipway 1 mile in Aberporth.

£££ 🐕 ⅲ M CL CS ① WiFi

Directions: Turn off A487 onto B4333 0.3 miles west of Tan-y-Groes sp 'Aberporth'. The site entrance is on the right in 1.25 miles. This route avoids narrow roads in the town centre.

GPS: N52°07.552' W004°31.761'
OS grid: 145 SN 270 505

April (or Easter if earlier) - October

Llety Caravan Park

Tresaith, Ceredigion, SA43 2ED
Tel: 01239 810354
www.lletycaravanpark.co.uk

Talywerydd Touring Caravan and Camping Park

Sarnau, Llandysul Ceredigion, SA44 6QY
Tel: 01239 810322
www.talyweryddcaravanpark.co.uk

Photo courtesy of Kerry Thomas

Set right on the cliffs between Aberporth and Tresaith, this site has a number of static caravans and seasonal pitches. Some touring pitches are right by the site entrance, others are on a partly sloping field with a wide view of Cardigan Bay. 8 fully serviced pitches are available, each having a water tap, a wastewater drain and hook-up. There is direct access to the Wales Coast Path making it just a short walk down to the beach at Tresaith and just over 1 mile in the other direction to Aberporth.

This small, traditional, family run campsite is set over three fields. Some pitches are slightly sloping and most have a good view over open countryside to Cardigan Bay. Onsite facilities are not new but are kept clean. This is a quiet rural location just a few mins drive from the beaches at Penbryn, Tresaith and Aberporth.

| NA 4 | NP 12 | 6/10 AMP | | |
| WC | | | | |

Disabled toilets a long way from touring pitches.

£££ WiFi

Directions: Turn off A487 onto B4333 0.3 miles west of Tan-y-Groes sp 'Aberporth'. As enter Aberporth, take the 1st right sp 'Tre-saith'. The site is on the left in 0.75 miles. This route avoids narrow roads in the town centre.

Cymru Wales
★★★★

GPS: N52°07.951' W004°31.397'
OS grid: 145 SN 274 513

March - October

| NA 6 | NP 40 | 16 AMP | | |
| WC | | | MG | MB |

Pub 2 miles. Farm shop 550m. Beach 1.75 miles. Slipway 3 miles.

££££ WiFi

Directions: Turn off A487 8.25 miles east of Cardigan sp 'Penbryn', 'Tresaith' and for the campsite. The site is on the left in 550m.

GPS: N52°07.742' W004°29.224'
OS grid: 145 SN 298 508

April (or Easter if earlier) - October

Ty Rhos Farm Campsite *CS*

New Quay, Llandysul, Ceredigion, SA45 9TU
Tel: 01545 560457
www.tyrhos.co.uk

This is an attractive, peaceful and well tended site on a mainly flat field with extensive, but distant, sea views. The 5 hardstanding pitches are for members only, but there is an additional 2 acre field with space for 15 tents and there is a gothic camping pod for hire. Although the site is in a rural location, the popular resort of New Quay is a 1 mile drive and access to the Wales Coast Path is less than 0.5 miles away.

| NA 2 | NP 20 | 8 AMP | | |

Pub, shop, beach and slipway 1 mile at New Quay.

£££

Directions: At Synod Inn, turn off A487 onto A486 sp 'New Quay'. Turn 1st left as you reach New Quay, immediately before the Penrhiwllan Inn. Follow the road for 0.75 miles and the site is on the left.

GPS: N52°12.353' W004°22.471'
OS grid: 145 SN 378 591

All year

Cei Bach Country Club Touring and Tenting Park

Parc-Y-Brwcs, Cei Bach, New Quay,
Ceredigion, SA45 9SL Tel: 01545 580237
www.cei-bach.co.uk

From an elevated position, this slightly sloping site overlooks Cei Bach Bay. The view is interspersed with mature trees but improves the further up the slope you pitch. The modern facilities and attractive landscape are well maintained. From the site campers can either follow a path down to a sheltered, sandy bathing beach or along the Welsh Coast Path to Aberaeron, passing over a waterfall on the way. The beautiful fishing village of New Quay with its resident family of dolphins is 1.5 miles away.

| NA 3 | NP 60 | 16 AMP | | |

Pub and shop 1 mile. Slipway 2 miles at New Quay.

£££

Directions: From A487 turn onto B4342 in Llanarth by the Llanina Arms pub sp 'New Quay'. After 2 miles, pass the Schooner Park caravan site and turn right at the crossroads sp 'Cei Bach'. Follow the narrow lane for 1 mile and then turn left sp 'Traeth Beach'. The site is 60m on the left.

GPS: N52°12.657' W004°19.873'
OS grid: 146 SN 408 595

March - October

Camping on the Farm

Drefnewydd Farm, Aberaeron, Ceredigion,
SA46 0JR Tel: 07773 769318
www.campingonthefarm.co.uk

This small, family run campsite has two flat fields set right on the coast with views of the sea over a protective bank. The Georgian harbour town of Aberaeron is 0.3 miles away and there is direct access onto the shingle beach.

| NA 6 | NP 50 | 💀 10 AMP | 🚐 | 🚐 |

| WC | ♿ | 🚿 | 🧺 | 🛁 | 🔲 | MG | MB |

🔲 🧹 🔍 🛥 ✂ 🛝 🚶

£££ 🐕 †† M CL CS ⓘ WiFi

Directions: The site is adjacent to A487 0.3 miles northeast of Aberaeron.

GPS: N52°14.709' W004°15.173'
OS grid: 146 SN 463 632

Easter - October

Morfa Farm

Llanrhystud, Ceredigion, SY23 5BU
Tel: 01974 202253
www.morfa.net

This family run caravan park is part of a working farm and extends over several flat fields with sea views from some pitches. Request a sea view pitch when booking if desired. There is also a large field available for rallies, groups or events. The site is adjacent to a river, fishing permitted, and a pebble beach with some sand. A tennis court and snooker room are available for use and the small onsite shop stocks essential groceries and frozen foods. To walk the 0.8 miles to Llanrhystud, join the Wales Coast Path at the end of the drive.

| NA 3 | NP 30 | 💀 10 AMP | 🚐 | 🚐 |

| WC | ♿ | 🚿 | 🧺 | 🛁 | 🔲 | MG | MB |

🔲 🧹 🔍 🛥 ✂ 🛝 🚶
Pub 1 mile.

££££ 🐕 †† M CL CS ⓘ WiFi

Directions: Turn off A487 south of Llanrhystud opposite the Gwasanaethau Services fuel station, there is an advert for the campsite in the trees. Follow the lane towards the beach. In 0.5 miles turn right into the farm road sp for the site.

GPS: N52°18.170' W004°09.608'
OS grid: 135 SN 528 694

April (or Easter if earlier) - October

Pengarreg Caravan Park 53

Llanrhystud, Ceredigion, SY23 5DJ
Tel: 01974 202247

On the opposite side of the river from Morfa Farm, all touring pitches on this site have good sea views thanks to the slightly elevated position above the pebble beach. The onsite shop is well stocked with essentials and there is a clubhouse a short stroll from touring area. The river Wyre runs adjacent to the park and offers 1 mile of private freshwater and sea trout fishing. Sea fishing trips are available from two nearby harbours. The village of Llanrhystud is 0.5 miles away.

| NA 15 | NP 60 | ☠ 16 AMP | | |

WC ⬚ ⬚ ⬚ ⬚ ⬚ MG MB

⬚ ⬚ ⬚ ⬚ ⬚ ⬚ ⬚

££££ 🐕 †† M CL CS ⓘ WiFi

Directions: Turn off A487 south of Llanrhystud opposite the Gwasanaethau Services fuel station. Turn immediately right into the entrance driveway sp 'Pengarreg Caravan Park'. Follow the driveway 0.5 miles to the caravan park.

GPS: N52°18.328' W004°09.357'
OS grid: 135 SN 530 697

March - January

Morfa Bychan Holiday Park 54

Llanfarian, Aberystwyth, Ceredigion, SY23 4QQ Tel: 01970 617254
www.hillandale.co.uk

The touring field on this well maintained holiday site has sheep pastures behind and has wide views over Cardigan Bay. Most touring pitches are sloping. There are good facilities and the attractive reception/shop has friendly, helpful staff and stocks basic essentials. The site has direct access to a private pebble beach where you can roam the rock pools, ride a few waves or try to catch bass. The Wales Coast Path runs just behind the site.

| NA 3 | NP 65 | ☠ 10 AMP | | |

WC ⬚ ⬚ ⬚ ⬚ ⬚ MG MB

⬚ ⬚ ⬚ ⬚ ⬚ ⬚ ⬚
Pub 2.5 miles at Llanfarian. Slipway 5 miles at Aberystwyth.

££££ 🐕 †† M CL CS ⓘ WiFi

Directions: The easiest access to the site is from the south. Turn off A487 0.5 miles south of Blaenplwyf and 4 miles north of Llanrhystud sp for the campsite. Follow sp for the campsite for 2 miles to the site. GPS given at last major turning.

GPS: N52°22.312' W004°05.828'
OS grid: 135 SN 565 770

April - September

Glan Y Môr Leisure Park

Clarach Bay, Aberystwyth, Ceredigion,
SY23 3DT Tel: 01970 828900
www.sunbourne.com

This large leisure park is situated right next to Clarach Bay beach. In addition to the statics, there are two separate touring areas. The one alongside the road has limited sea views, but the other is well located above the main site and has excellent views of the bay. This full facilities park has everything from an indoor heated swimming pool to bowling lanes. Make the most of the scenery by taking a ride on the Vale of Rheidol Railway, a 12 mile, 1 hour long journey from Aberystwyth to Devil's Bridge where you can see 90m waterfalls and traverse bridges set over a stunning woodland gorge.

| NA | 15 | NP | 150 | 16 AMP | | |

| WC | | | | | | MG | MB |

Slipway 4.5 miles at Borth.

£££ WiFi

Directions: Turn off A487 in Bow Street sp 'Llangorwen' and 'Clarach'. In 1.5 miles go straight over the crossroads and the site is in 1 mile at the end of the road.

GPS: N52°26.168' W004°04.820'
OS grid: 135 SN 587 840

March - October

Ocean View Holiday Park

North Beach, Clarach Bay, Aberystwyth, SY23
3DT Tel: 01970 828425
www.oceanviewholidays.com

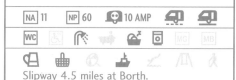

This holiday park accommodates mostly statics, but the few touring pitches available do have sea views over the statics. The facilities are clean and conveniently located for the touring field. A short walk from the park is Clarach Bay's sand and shale beach which offers safe swimming and rock pooling. Seafront commerce includes a supermarket, restaurant, take-away and pub. The camera obscura on the summit of Constitution Hill is well worth a visit. The Wales Coast Path passes along the shore.

| NA | 11 | NP | 60 | 10 AMP | | |

| WC | | | | | | MG | MB |

Slipway 4.5 miles at Borth.

£££ WiFi

Directions: Turn off A487 in Bow Street sp 'Llangorwen' and 'Clarach'. In 1.5 miles go straight over the crossroads and the site is on the right in 0.5 miles.

GPS: N52°26.181' W004°04.429'
OS grid: 135 SN 591 841

March - October

Cae-Du Campsite

Cae-Du, Rhoslefain, Tywyn,
Gwynedd, LL36 9ND
Tel: 01654 711234

This site's wonderful location makes it perfect to get away from it all. Divided into several areas, some pitches are almost on the beach with others at higher levels, but all have a fine view of the sea. The facilities are modern and well kept which is a pleasure to find on such an informal site. There is a very relaxed atmosphere and open fires are allowed. The site is 500m from the Wales Coast Path.

NA 10 | NP 70 | 0 AMP

WC | MG | MB

Pub 3 miles. Shop 4 miles at Bryncrug.
Slipway 7 miles at Tywyn.

£££

Directions: The site is adjacent to A493 where it bends north along the coast, 0.6 miles west of Rhoslefain and 13.25 miles south of the junction with A470. Entry is down a steep, rough track passing under a narrow railway bridge. Stop at the farm to book in. If coming from Aberdyfi with a motorhome or caravan, it's better to go past the site and turn around in the next lay-by.

GPS: N52°37.992' W004°06.971'
OS grid: 124 SH 569 059

Easter - October

Bwlchgwyn Farm

Arthog, Dolgellau, LL39 1BX
Tel: 01341 250103
www.bwlchgwynfarm.co.uk

Situated next to the Arthog Outdoor Education Centre, this hillside farm site is set high above the Mawddach Estuary with commanding views of Barmouth Bay from the terraced pitches. Most pitches are level and firm, but those on the highest part of the site are sloping. The portable toilet and shower facilities are basic, but adequate and clean. Pony trekking is available at the farm. Fairbourne, 1 mile, is a small resort with a Blue Flag beach and narrow gauge steam railway.

NA 4 | NP 30 | 16 AMP

WC | MG | MB

Pub, shop, beach and slipway 1 mile.

£££

Directions: The farm is just off A493 0.5 miles north of the turn off to Fairbourne and the beach. Turn off A493 sp for the farm and 'Arthog Outdoor Education Centre'. Go up the drive for 180m and check in at the farmhouse on the left.

GPS: N52°41.977' W004°02.342'
OS grid: 124 SH 625 134

Easter - September

Graig Wen

Arthog, Dolgellau, LL39 1BQ
Tel: 01341 250482
www.graigwen.co.uk

Graig Wen is well located high above the Mawddach Estuary. From parts of the site there are extensive views over wetlands to the mouth of the estuary making it a great birdwatching base. The top part of the site is flat and accommodates tents and tourers. During summer there is another extensive and beautifully isolated area made available for tents at £8 per person. This wooded oasis is down the hill and through the woods towards the river, but it's a long walk back up to the showers and toilets! The popular Mawddach Trail is directly accessible from the lower part of the site.

| NA | 45 | NP | 36 | ☠ 16 AMP | | |

| WC | | | | | | |

Pub, shop, beach and slipway 4 miles.

£££

Directions: This site is adjacent to A493 3.5 miles north of Fairbourne. It is a tight turn into the site if approaching from Fairbourne in the south, therefore users of larger vehicles should approach from A470 in the north. Turn off A470 sp 'Tywyn A493'. Follow road for 4.5 miles and the site is on the right.

GPS: N52°43.360' W003°59.550'
OS grid: 124 SH 654 157

March - January

Tyddyn Du

Bontddu, Dolgellau, LL40 2UA
Tel: 01341 430644
www.freewebs.com/tyddyndu

This informal site is located right alongside the Mawddach Estuary a short distance inland from Barmouth. There are views right down to the estuary to the west and to Cadair Idris to the south from parts of the site. The site is partly in ancient oak woods and partly on flat land adjacent to the river, so the lower lying sections may be unusable when wet. Facilities are quite basic and probably inadequate if the site is busy. Electric hook-up is available upon request. Open fires are allowed as long as the wood burnt is purchased on site.

| NA | 8 | NP | 110 | ☠ 16 AMP | | |

| WC | | | | | | |

Pub, shop, beach and slipway 5 miles at Barmouth.

£££

Directions: The site is adjacent to A496 exactly halfway between Barmouth and Dolgellau.

GPS: N52°44.834' W003°58.614'
OS grid: 124 SH 668 184

April (or Easter if earlier) - October

Caerddaniel Holiday Home Park 61

Llanaber, Barmouth, LL42 1RR
Tel: 01341 280611
www.caerddaniel.co.uk

This static caravan park has four camping areas for tents, two at the top of the park and two at the bottom. The top areas are on a steeper gradient while the bottom areas are on a gentler slope, but all have unrestricted views of the sea. The majority of the pitches cannot be reserved, but there are a few with electric hook-up which must be booked in advance. There is an onsite shop with a take-away. Barmouth Bay's huge sandy beach is just across the railway line and is accessed via a gated level crossing. Barmouth is 2.25 miles away with shops, pubs, cafés and a harbour.

NA	20	NP	150	16 AMP

Boat launching facilities on site.

£££ WiFi

Directions: The site is adjacent to A496 2.25 miles north of Barmouth.

GPS: N52°44.963' W004°04.722'
OS grid: 124 SH 597 188

Easter - September

Trawsdir Touring Caravans and Camping Park 62

Llanaber, Barmouth, LL42 1RR
Tel: 01341 280999
www.trawsdir.co.uk

This high quality site is attractively laid out on terraces ensuring that most pitches have a good view of the sea. Motorhome and caravan pitches are on gravel and tents are accommodated in a field next to the main road with additional space above the terraces. The impressive reception/facilities building is modern and all of the facilities are of an excellent standard. The site employs solar water heating and photovoltaic panels and a wind turbine to generate energy. They aim to be 50% self sufficient in energy consumption and there is a live display in reception showing their progress.

NA	10	NP	100	16 AMP

Beach 0.5 miles.

£££ WiFi

Directions: The site is adjacent to A496 2.5 miles north of Barmouth.

GPS: N52°45.426' W004°04.978'
OS grid: 124 SH 596 197

March - January

Tyddyn Goronwy Camping Park 63

Fford Glan Mor, Tal Y Bont, LL43 2AQ
Tel: 01341 247632
www.tyddyngoronwy.co.uk

This is the only site in the Sunnysands group that caters solely for tourers, accommodating tents, caravans and motorhomes in three mainly flat fields. One of the fields has views of the sea over hedges. The huge beach of Barmouth Bay is 0.5 miles' walk. A free leisure pass entitles campers to use all the facilities at Sunnysands (bar, club, heated pool, etc) which is 0.75 miles' walk along the beach or 1 mile by car. The Wales Coast Path runs very close to the site.

| NA 10 | NP 70 | 16 AMP | | |

| WC | | | | | | MG | MB |

Swimming pool 1 mile at Sunnysands.

££££ 🐕 ♦♦ M CL CS (i) WiFi

Directions: Turn off A496 in Tal Y Bont 4 miles north of Barmouth sp with a campsite symbol and for the railway station. The site is on the left after crossing the railway bridge.

GPS: N52°46.353' W004°05.901'
OS grid: 124 SH 585 215

April - October

Shell Island 64

Llanbedr, LL45 2PJ
Tel: 01341 241453
www.shellisland.co.uk

Europe's largest campsite! The site is huge, covering nearly 400 acres, so there is plenty of room for everyone to spread out over the many different pitching areas. There are no allocated pitches and you can pitch up right next to the beach, in the sand dunes, in a grassy field, alongside a small harbour, on top of a hill, or in a sheltered dip. Main facilities are in a central complex which houses the supermarket, gift shop, launderette, snack bar, restaurant, bar and games room. Toilets and showers are here also, with additional toilets located around the site. Note that there are no electric hook ups and caravans are not accepted.

| NA 380 | NP 800 | 0 AMP | | |

| WC | | | | | | MG | MB |

££££ 🐕 ♦♦ M CL CS (i) WiFi

Directions: In Llanbedr, turn off A496 at the river bridge sp 'Shell Island' and for the railway station. Follow the road for 2.25 miles to the campsite. There is a tidal causeway as you approach the site which is impassable during some high tides.

GPS: N52°49.079' W004°08.556'
OS grid: 124 SH 556 266

March - October

Argoed Campsite and *CL*

Llanbedr, LL45 2HS
Tel: 01341 241723
www.argoedfarmholidays.com

This farm site has a wide view over Cardigan Bay to the sea from the 5 non member pitches and more limited views from the 5 CL pitches which are set further back. The showers and toilets are attractively located within the metre wide stone walls of a former farm building. The nearest beach is 0.75 miles away and is accessible via a footpath just across the main road. The site is surrounded by footpaths which lead into the hills or join the Wales Coast Path. Larger motorhomes can sometimes be accepted on site, but space must be confirmed in advance.

| NA | 2.5 | NP | 15 | 6 AMP | | |

| WC | | | | | MG | MB |

Pub and shop 1 mile. Beach 0.75 miles. Slipway 0.5 miles.

£££ ★ ♦♦ M *CL* CS ⓘ WiFi

Directions: The site is adjacent to A496 between Llanfair and Llanbedr, 2 miles south of Harlech.

GPS: N52°50.061' W004°06.577'
OS grid: 124 SH 579 284

Easter - October

Merthyr Farm Campsite

Harlech, LL46 2TP
Tel: 01766 780897
www.merthyrfarm.co.uk

The site is set high in the hills above Harlech on a 350 acre working hill farm. It is a quiet, peaceful location with outstanding panoramic views out to sea over Tremadog Bay to the west, and all the way to Snowdon to the north on a clear day. Being fairly high and exposed, this can be a windy site! The well appointed shower, toilet, laundry and washing up facilities are located in converted farm buildings.

| NA | 4 | NP | 25 | 16 AMP | | |

| WC | | | | | MG | MB |

Pub, shop and beach 2.5 miles.

£££ ★ ♦♦ M *CL* CS ⓘ WiFi

Directions: 1 mile south of Harlech, turn off A496 away from the sea and opposite sp 'Llandanwg'. After 230m turn left at the crossroads, then take the 2nd right just before the white bungalow. Continue on this road for 2.25 miles. Turn left sp 'Fferm Merthyr' and cross a cattle grid. In 360m turn into the farm gateway set in a stone wall on the left.

GPS: N52°51.981' W004°04.732'
OS grid: 124 SH 601 318

May - October

Mynydd Du Holiday Park

Porthmadog Road, Criccieth, LL52 0PS
Tel: 07407 646877
www.mynydddu.co.uk

This partly sloping site has great sea and mountain views from most areas. The touring pitches are amongst seasonal caravans and a large tenting field is behind. There are some fully serviced touring pitches available which can be requested when booking. The modern toilet and shower facilities are housed in attractive timber chalet style buildings. The site is just 1.25 miles from the small seaside resort of Criccieth with its 13th century castle. No holiday in this area would be complete without a day trip to Portmeirion, 7.5 miles away.

| NA 8 | NP 80 | 16 AMP | | |

Pub, shop and beach 1 mile at Criccieth.

£££

Directions: The site is adjacent to A497, 1.25 miles east of Criccieth.

GPS: N52°55.675' W004°12.490'
OS grid: 123 SH 515 393

March - October

Eisteddfa Caravan and Camping Park

Pentrefelin, Criccieth, LL52 0PT
Tel: 01766 522696
www.eisteddfapark.co.uk

This attractive hillside site offers good views over Cardigan Bay from the top section. The rest of the site offers views of the surrounding hills. There are terraced touring pitches as well as statics, seasonal pitches and grass areas for tents. Request a pitch with a sea view when booking if desired. The site also has two fully equipped tipis and a camping cocoon. Eisteddfa Fisheries is adjacent to the site, www.eisteddfa-fisheries.com, which has five lakes for carp, fly and family fishing.

| NA 11 | NP 120 | 10 AMP | | |

Pub, shop, beach and slipway 1.5 miles at Criccieth.

£££

Directions: The site is adjacent to A497 1.5 miles east of Criccieth.

GPS: N52°55.816' W004°12.222'
OS grid: 123 SH 518 392

March - October

Sarn Farm Caravan and Camping Site [69]

Sarn Bach, Abersoch, Pwllheli, LL53 7BG
Tel: 01758 713583

This family run site is set over two partly sloping fields with a view to the sea from most pitches. Toilet and shower facilities are clean and well maintained. Footpaths lead to beaches on the east and west side of the peninsula. The large sandy beach at St Tudwal's Road is 0.75 miles and runs all the way to Abersoch. A walk along the Wales Coast Path south of the beach will give you a good view of Bear Grylls' private island, St Tudwal's Island West. Abersoch centre is just 1.25 miles away with small shops, bars, restaurants and cafés.

| NA | 5.5 | NP | 60 | | 10 AMP | | |

| WC | | | | | | | |

| | | | | | | | |
Pub, shop, beach and slipway 0.75 miles.

£££ 🐕 ♂♀ M CL CS ⓘ WiFi

Directions: Follow A499 to Abersoch. In Abersoch follow sp 'Sarn Bach' on the one-way system. Continue south for 0.9 miles to Sarn Bach. 110m past Sarn Bach Caravan Park, turn off between houses sp 'Sarn Bach Farm'.

Cymru Wales
★★★

GPS: N52°48.645' W004°31.012'
OS grid: 123 SH 305 266

Easter - October

Beach View Caravan and Camping Park [70]

Bwlchtocyn, Abersoch, LL53 7BT
Tel: 01758 721956

(max 6.5m)

This partly sloping site is immaculately kept and has a good view over to Abersoch Bay from some pitches. The site mainly accommodates seasonal caravans, but has a few touring pitches available. Request a pitch with a sea view when booking if desired. A sandy beach with a slipway is just 0.25 miles down the hill. The beach runs all the way to Abersoch which is popular for water sports. Abersoch centre is just 1 mile away with small shops, bars, restaurants and cafés.

| NA | 4 | NP | 47 | | 16 AMP | | |

| WC | | | | | | | |

| | | | | | | | |
Pub and shop 1.5 miles. Slipway 0.25 miles.

£££ 🐕 ♂♀ M CL CS ⓘ WiFi

Directions: Follow A499 to Abersoch. In Abersoch follow sp 'Sarn Bach' on the one-way system. Continue south through Sarn Bach for 1.5 miles. Turn left sp 'Bwlchtocyn' and 'Gwesty Porth Tocyn Hotel' and after 0.5 miles turn left again sp 'Gwesty Porth Tocyn Hotel'. The site is on the left in 0.25 miles.

Cymru Wales
★★★

GPS: N52°48.402' W004°30.153'
OS grid: 123 SH 313 261

March - October

Bryn Bach Caravan and Campsite 71

Tyddyn Talgoch Uchaf, Bwlchtocyn,
Abersoch, LL53 7BT Tel: 01758 712285
www.abersochcamping.co.uk

(max 8m)

Bryn Bach is a family run site providing seasonal and touring pitches with excellent views over Abersoch Bay. The site is partly sloping, but level pitches are available. A 0.5 miles' walk downhill, or a 0.75 miles' drive, will take you to a sandy beach. The beach runs all the way to Abersoch which is popular for water sports. Abersoch centre is 1 mile along the beach or 2 miles' drive and has small shops, bars, restaurants and cafés.

| NA 3 | NP 36 | 16 AMP | | |

| WC | | | | | MG | MB |

Pub, shop and slipway 2 miles. Beach 0.5 miles.

£££ WiFi

Directions: Follow A499 to Abersoch. In Abersoch follow sp 'Sarn Bach' on the one-way system. Continue south through Sarn Bach for 1.5 miles. Turn left sp 'Bwlchtocyn' and 'Gwesty Porth Tocyn Hotel' and the site is sp in 0.75 miles on the left.

GPS: N52°48.167' W004°30.055'
OS grid: 123 SH 315 257

March - October

Cilan Fawr Campsite CS 72

Cilan, Abersoch, Pwllheli, LL53 7DD
Tel: 01758 713276
www.abersochholidays.net

This isolated site is set on a partly sloping field with distant sea views over Hells Mouth Bay. The associated riding centre is open during the summer and caters for children, novice and experienced riders. The adjoining 250 acres of open access land provides plenty of opportunity for safe off-road riding.

| NA 5 | NP 25 | 10 AMP | | |

| WC | | | | | MG | MB |

Pub and shop 3 miles.

££ M CS

Directions: Follow A499 to Abersoch. In Abersoch follow sp 'Sarn Bach' on the one-way system. Continue south through Sarn Bach for 2.25 miles. Bear right at a remote bungalow onto road marked 'Unsuitable for heavy goods vehicles' and the farmhouse is in 0.5 miles immediately before a cattle grid. Cross the grid, turn left and park, then book in at the farmhouse.

GPS: N52°47.600' W004°31.789'
OS grid: 123 SH 295 247

Easter - October

Garreg Haul *CS* 〔73〕

Cilan, Abersoch, Pwllheli, LL53 7DD
Tel: 01758 710092

🏕 🚐 🚙 🚌 🚐

This isolated site is set on a partly sloping field with an excellent sea view to Hells Mouth Bay. The nearby riding centre is open during the summer and caters for children, novice and experienced riders. The adjoining 250 acres of open access land provides plenty of opportunity for safe off-road riding.

| NA 2 | NP 35 | 💀 16 AMP | | |

| WC | | | | | | |

Pub and shop 3 miles.

££ 🐕 †† M CL CS ⓘ WiFi

Directions: Follow A499 to Abersoch. In Abersoch follow sp 'Sarn Bach' on the one-way system. Continue south through Sarn Bach for 2.25 miles. Bear right at a remote bungalow onto road marked 'Unsuitable for heavy goods vehicles', then continue 0.5 miles, cross a cattle grid and continue straight along the level track. Bear right in 140m, then bear left and follow the track to the site. If in doubt, ask at Cilan Fawr farmhouse by the cattle grid.

GPS: N52°47.734' W004°32.032'
OS grid: 123 SH 292 250

March - October

Deucoch Touring and Camping Park 〔74〕

Sarn Bach, Abersoch, Pwllheli, LL53 7LD
Tel: 01758 713293
www.deucoch.com

🏕 🚐 🚙 🚌 🚐

Deucoch is a good quality, well cared for site with both seasonal and touring pitches. Most pitches have a fine sea view over Abersoch Bay. The facilities are excellent, including free indoor and outdoor showers. Popular for water sports, Abersoch centre is 1.25 miles and has small shops, bars, restaurants and cafés.

| NA 5 | NP 30 | 💀 10 AMP | | |

| WC | ♿ | | | | MG | |

£££ 🐕 †† M CL CS ⓘ WiFi

Directions: Follow A499 to Abersoch. In Abersoch follow sp 'Sarn Bach' on the one-way system. Continue south for 0.7 miles, passing the 1st right turn sp for the campsite, and turn right at the next crossroads in Sarn Bach sp 'Llanengan'. Follow road around to the left, past the school, and the site is sp on the right.

Cymru Wales
★★★★

GPS: N52°48.771' W004°31.254'
OS grid: 123 SH 302 268

March - October

Trem-Y-Mor Touring Park

Sarn Bach, Abersoch, Pwllheli, LL53 7ET
Tel: 07967 050170
www.tgholidays.co.uk

This sloping site mainly accommodates seasonal caravans, but the level, terraced touring pitches at the top of the site have good views over Abersoch Bay. Shower and toilet facilities are of a very good standard. A large sandy beach with a slipway is 1 mile away. Footpaths lead to beaches on the east and west side of the peninsula. The large sandy beach at St Tudwal's Road is 0.75 miles and runs all the way to Abersoch.

| NA 4 | NP 53 | 10 AMP | | |

Pub, shop, beach and slipway all 1 mile.

£££

Directions: Follow A499 to Abersoch. In Abersoch follow sp 'Sarn Bach' on the one-way system. Continue south for 1.2 miles to Sarn Bach. Drive past Sarn Bach Caravan Park and Sarn Bach Farm and turn left at crossroads sp 'Trem-Y-Mor Touring Park'. The site is in 140m.

GPS: N52°48.604' W004°30.897'
OS grid: 123 SH 306 265

March - October

Tyn-Y-Mur
Touring and Camping Park

Lon Garmon, Abersoch, Pwllheli, LL53 7UL
Tel: 01758 712328
www.tyn-y-mur.co.uk

Set high above Abersoch, this open site has views to the sea in two directions ensuring that most pitches benefit from sea views. The site is divided into two main sections, one mainly accommodating seasonal caravans and the other for tourers and tenters. There is also a large area set aside as a football pitch which is popular with younger campers. The adjacent 'hidden valley' is a great place to explore and also provides river fishing. Abersoch is 1 mile away.

| NA 4 | NP 55 | 20 AMP | | |

Beach and slipway 1.25 miles.

£££ WiFi

Directions: Follow A499 to Abersoch. Before you enter the town turn right sp 'Llangian'. Follow this road for 0.9 miles and the site is in on the left.

Cymru Wales
★★★★

GPS: N52°49.884' W004°31.392'
OS grid: 123 SH 301 289

March - October

Treheli Farm Campsite

Treheli, Rhiw, Pwllheli, Gwynedd, LL53 8AA
Tel: 01758 780281

This is one of those sites that people return to time and time again safe in the knowledge that it will still be a back to basics campsite with a relaxed atmosphere and stunning, uninterrupted views right across Hells Mouth Bay. The very basic facilities are adjacent to the farmhouse where there is also a spring water tap. Open fires are allowed. A steep walk leads down to the beach, a long stretch of sand and stones, which is exposed to the full force of the Atlantic. Though popular with surfers, the beach seldom gets busy. Note that bathing can be dangerous here with strong undertows and cross currents.

NA	1.5	NP	27		

Pub 4 miles at Abersoch. Slipway 4 miles at Aberdaron.

££££

Directions: From northeast on A499 turn onto B4413 in Llanberdrog sp 'Aberdaron'. Follow road for 2.4 miles through Mynytho, then turn left sp 'Rhiw'. Continue for 3.8 miles until you reach a crossroads. Continue straight and take the next left. Call at the farmhouse before pitching.

GPS: N52°49.541' W004°36.783'
OS grid: 123 SH 239 285

March - October

Morfa Mawr Farm

Aberdaron, Pwllheli, LL53 8BD
Tel: 01758 760264

This farm site is spread over two fields which lie a mere 200m from the beach. The larger of the two fields is flat and both have fabulous views over Aberdaron Bay. The facilities are maintained to a good standard. The site owners also run Morfa Bach campsite which is 0.5 miles west. There is direct beach access downhill and the sandy beach runs for 0.6 miles to Aberdaron which has a pub, café, and shop.

NA	3	NP	50	16 AMP	

Pub, shop and slipway 0.5 miles at Aberdaron.

£££

Directions: From Aberdaron, travel east on the coastal road sp 'Rhiw'. The farmhouse is in 0.6 miles on the left, book in there before pitching. The track across the road leads to the camping field.

GPS: N52°48.333' W004°41.842'
OS grid: 123 SH 182 262

March - October

Caerau Farm

Aberdaron, Pwllheli, LL53 8BG
Tel: 01758 760481

Dwyros
Caravan and Camping Site

Aberdaron, Pwllheli, LL53 8BS
Tel: 01758 760295

This traditional farm campsite is set over two fields with good sea views from most places. An additional tent field is located closer to the village. Facilities are not new, but are serviceable. Aberdaron is just 0.5 miles away with a pub, café, shop and sandy beach. The Wales Coast Path is 300m away as it passes through Aberdaron.

Set in open fields high above Aberdaron, this site has superb sea views over the bay taking in the islands of Ynys Gwylan-Fawr and Ynys Gwylan-Bach. Dwyros is a high quality campsite with excellent facilities. There is access to the beach via the Wales Coast Path across the road. The centre of Aberdaron is 0.5 miles where there is a pub, café, shop and a sandy beach.

NA 6	NP 60	10 AMP	
WC			

Pub, shop, beach and slipway all under 0.5 miles.

NA 6	NP 30	16 AMP	
WC			MG	MB

Pub, shop, beach and slipway 0.5 miles at Aberdaron.

££

£££

Directions: From A499 turn onto B4413 sp 'Aberdaron' and follow to Aberdaron. The site entrance is sp on the left just before you enter the village.

Directions: From northeast on A499 turn onto B4413 in Llanberdrog sp 'Aberdaron' with a campsite symbol. Follow road for 12.7 miles into Aberdaron. Pass the Spar shop on the left and take the next right just before the bridge sp 'Playground'. The site is up the hill is in 0.5 miles on the right.

GPS: N52°48.600' W004°42.486'
OS grid: 123 SH 175 268

GPS: N52°48.303' W004°43.169'
OS grid: 123 SH 167 266

March - October

March - October

Mynydd Mawr Camping and Caravan Site 81

Llanllawen Fawr, Aberdaron, Pwllheli, LL53 8BY
Tel: 01758 760223
www.aberdaroncaravanandcampingsite.co.uk

This gloriously isolated and informal site is located amongst rolling hills on the edge of a National Trust protected area. There are wonderful views in all directions and sea views in two directions. There are two fields, one flat and one partly sloping. The facilities, although basic, are clean and well kept with the unexpected bonus of two family bathrooms. An onsite café serves breakfast, afternoon tea with home made cakes, refreshments and ice cream. There is reputed to be good fishing off the rocks a short walk from the site and the adjoining National Trust headland is a popular attraction for walkers.

| NA | 1.25 | NP | 30 | 6 AMP | | |

| WC | | | | | | MG | MB |

Pub, shop, beach and slipway 2 miles at Aberdaron.

££££

Directions: From north on B4413, turn right off B4413 3.25 miles beyond Pen-Y-Groeslon sp 'Uwchmynydd'. Follow road for 1 mile, then turn right sp 'Uwchmynydd'. Continue down the narrow road for 1.4 miles further, passing a chapel on the right. The site is 0.25 miles beyond Ty Newydd Farm campsite.

GPS: N52°47.703' W004°45.353'
OS grid: 123 SH 143 255

March - October

Ty-Newydd Farm Caravan and Camping Site 82

Uwchmynydd, Aberdaron, Pwllheli, LL53 8BY
Tel: 01758 760581
www.tynewyddfarm-site.co.uk

This tidy and well cared for site has sea views from some pitches across to Bardsey Island, but these should be requested when booking if desired. The shower and toilet facilities are very good and the small café serves all day breakfasts and afternoon cream teas. The site is popular with families, and walkers will find the location ideal as much of the coast is owned by the National Trust. Boat trips to Barsdey Island may be taken when sea conditions allow.

| NA | 5 | NP | 60 | 6 AMP | | |

| WC | | | | | | MG | MB |

Pub, shop, beach and slipway 2 miles at Aberdaron.

££££

Directions: From north on B4413, turn right off B4413 3.25 miles beyond Pen-Y-Groeslon sp 'Uwchmynydd'. Follow road for 1 mile, then turn right sp 'Uwchmynydd'. Continue down the narrow road for 1.2 miles further, passing a chapel on the right. Enter the site on the left via a sharp turn. Users of large vehicles should phone in advance as alternative access can be arranged if required.

Cymru Wales
★★★

GPS: N52°47.827' W004°45.090'
OS grid: 123 SH 146 257

March - October

Plasffordd *CL*	83

Plasffordd, Aberdaron, Pwllheli, LL53 8LL
Tel: 01758 760439

This is a flat site with a distant view of the sea. This site is quiet, secluded and very reasonably priced. The owner's house is across the road, where a toilet and shower are available. Access to a rocky cove is 0.5 miles via a footpath and the beach at Whistling Sands is 1 mile by road.

NA	0.75	NP	5	16 AMP		
WC						

Pub, shop, beach and slipway 1 mile at Aberdaron.

££££ 🐕 ♟ M *CL* CS ⓘ WiFi

Directions: From north on B4413, turn right off B4413 3.25 miles beyond Pen-Y-Groeslon sp 'Uwchmynydd'. In 0.6 miles turn right sp 'Whistling Sands' and 'Anelog'. Follow road for 1.1 miles and the site entrance is straight ahead as the road bends right.

GPS: N52°49.299' W004°43.728'
OS grid: 123 SH 162 284

April - October

Morawel Caravan and Camping Site	84

Morawel, Aberdaron, Pwllheli, LL53 8BL
Tel: 01758 760408

The site is set on a partly sloping field behind houses which partly obscure the view to the sea over Aberdaron. Facilities are rather old and run down, but it is one of the cheaper sites in the area. Aberdaron is 0.75 miles downhill and has a sandy beach, shop, pub and café.

NA	2	NP	20	16 AMP		
WC						

Pub, shop, beach and slipway 1 mile.

££££ 🐕 ♟ M CL CS ⓘ WiFi

Directions: From northeast on A499 turn onto B4413 in Llanberdrog sp 'Aberdaron'. Follow road for 11.75 miles towards Aberdaron. The site entrance is adjacent to B4413 on the right 0.7 miles north of Aberdaron.

GPS: N52°48.792' W004°42.275'
OS grid: 123 SH 178 274

March - October

Llecyn Llangwnadl

Llangwnadl, Pwllheli, LL53 8NT
Tel: 01758 770347

Located on a working farm, this is a tidy and basic family site with a view of the sea over the hedges. The beautiful and isolated Penllech Beach and the Wales Coast Path are 0.5 miles down the footpath opposite the site entrance.

NA 4   NP 35   6 AMP

WC

Shop 0.25 mile and 3 miles. Slipway 0.25 miles.

££££

Directions: From Pwllheli, take A497 north sp 'Nefyn'. After 5 miles go straight over the roundabout adjacent to the Y Bryncynan Inn onto B4412 sp 'Morfa Nefyn'. In the village, turn left onto B4417 sp 'Aberdaron'. Follow B4417 for 7 miles, then turn right sp 'Llangwnnadl' and 'Porth colmon'. Follow sp 'Porth colmon' down the narrow lane and the site is on the left in 1.25 miles.

GPS: N52°52.271' W004°40.816'
OS grid: 123 SH 197 338

Easter - October

Penrallt Coastal Campsite

Tudweiliog, Pwllheli, LL53 8PB
Tel: 01758 770654
www.penrallt.co.uk

Penrallt is a family campsite set over several flat fields, but the 'Seaview Field' is the only one with a decent view of the sea and it is used mainly by tents. The site has been awarded Green Dragon Accreditation from the Welsh Assembly and Gold Standard from the Marine Conservation Society for commitment to environmental sustainability. Onsite facilities are good but quirky. The rocky shore is a couple of mins walk and 15 mins walk along the Wales Coast Path will take you to a sandy beach.

NA 4   NP 40   5/10 AMP

WC

Pub and shop 1 mile.

£££

Directions: From Pwllheli, take A497 north sp 'Nefyn'. After 5 miles go straight over the roundabout adjacent to the Y Bryncynan Inn onto B4412 sp 'Morfa Nefyn'. In the village, turn left onto B4417 sp 'Aberdaron'. Follow B4417 for 4.6 miles. 0.5 miles after Tudweiliog village turn right sp for the campsite. Follow this road for 0.8 miles and turn right just past a long, stone bungalow sp for the campsite. The site is in 0.4 miles.

GPS: N52°53.660' W004°39.288'
OS grid: 123 SH 215 362

April (or Easter if earlier) - September

Tan Llan Camping and Caravan Site `87`

Tudweiliog, Pwllheli, LL53 8AQ
Tel: 01758 770486
www.llynholiday.co.uk

This farm based site is flat and most pitches offer sea views across fields. There are separate fields for seasonal pitches, tourers, and tents. The shower and toilet facilities are located in converted farm buildings and are kept very clean. A small sandy beach is 0.75 miles by foot and the village of Tudweiliog is just 0.25 miles away where you can relax at the Lion Hotel which offers tasty food and good beer.

| NA 7 | NP 24 | 6/16 AMP | | |

| WC | | | | | |

Pub, shop and beach 0.75 miles. Slipway 4 miles.

££££ 🐕 ♦♦ M CL CS ⓘ WiFi

Directions: From Pwllheli, take A497 north sp 'Nefyn'. After 5 miles go straight over the roundabout adjacent to the Y Bryncynan Inn onto B4412 sp 'Morfa Nefyn'. In the village, turn left onto B4417 sp 'Aberdaron'. Follow B4417 for 3.75 miles and the site is adjacent to B4417 on the left.

GPS: N52°54.141' W004°37.170'
OS grid: 123 SH 239 370

April - October

Pant Gwyn Farm *CL* `88`

Tudweiliog, Pwllheli, LL53 8PE
Tel: 01758 770302

This farm site has 5 caravan and motorhome pitches for members in one small field and a separate field accommodates 5 non-member tents. Both fields have sea views over hedges but the views are better from the tent field. The facilities are kept very clean. From site you can walk 0.25 miles along a footpath to the rocky shore where the Wales Coast Path can be followed southwest for a further 0.5 miles to a small sandy beach.

| NA 1 | NP 10 | 10 AMP | | |

| WC | | | | | |

Pub, shop and beach 1 mile.

££££ 🐕 ♦♦ M CL CS ⓘ WiFi

Directions: From Pwllheli, take A497 north sp 'Nefyn'. After 5 miles go straight over the roundabout adjacent to the Y Bryncynan Inn onto B4412 sp 'Morfa Nefyn'. In the village, turn left onto B4417 sp 'Aberdaron'. Follow B4417 for 3.7 miles, then turn right next to a stone wall. Follow road 0.75 miles to the site.

GPS: N52°54.770' W004°37.084'
OS grid: 123 SH 240 382

April (or Easter if earlier) - October

Hirdre Fawr Farm

Tudweiliog, Pwllheli, LL53 8YY
Tel: 01758 770309
www.hirdrefawr.co.uk

Set on a working farm, this flat site is spread over four fields. There are sea views from the tent field and distant views from some other pitches, so a sea view pitch should be requested when booking if desired. Other pitches have views of the Yr Eifl Mountains. The shower and toilet facilities are to a very good standard. The site has private access to Rhosgor beach and the Wales Coast Path which is 0.75 miles' walk.

NA	10	NP	40	6/16 AMP		
WC						

Pub, shop, beach and slipway 1 mile.

£££

Directions: From Pwllheli, take A497 north sp 'Nefyn'. After 5 miles go straight over the roundabout adjacent to the Y Bryncynan Inn onto B4412 sp 'Morfa Nefyn'. In the village, turn left onto B4417 sp 'Aberdaron'. Follow B4417 for 2.75 miles and the site is sp on the right.

GPS: N52°54.671' W004°36.244'
OS grid: 123 SH 249 380

April (or Easter if earlier) - October

Wern Caravan and Camping Site

Nefyn, Pwllheli, LL53 6LW
Tel: 01758 720432

This basic farm-based site is set on a partly sloping field with a good sea view. There is access to the pebbly beach via the footpath through the static caravan park just across the road from the campsite. Nefyn is 1.25 miles away and has local commerce and a maritime museum. The Wales Coast path runs behind the site and links to several other footpaths, one of which leads you on a 2.4 mile circular walk up and around Garn Boduan, an Iron Age hill fort which still has remnants of 100 round houses.

NA	2	NP	60	6 AMP		
WC					MG	MB

Pub, shop, beach and slipway 1.25 miles at Nefyn.

££££

Directions: From Pwllheli, take A497 north sp 'Nefyn'. After 5 miles turn right at the roundabout adjacent to the Y Bryncynan Inn to stay on A497. Follow A497 into Nefyn and onto B4417 and continue for 0.8 miles. The site is sp on the right opposite a static caravan park.

GPS: N52°56.632' W004°30.517'
OS grid: 123 SH 315 414

March - October

Penisarlon Farm Camping Site

Pistyll, Pwllheli, LL53 6LR
Tel: 01758 721533
www.penisarlonfarm.co.uk

There are excellent sea views from every part of this basic west-facing site which is set over three small fields. It is mainly sloping, but there are some terraced areas providing 8 pitches which are more or less level. Adventurous people can scramble down to a small rocky cove. Sandy or pebble beaches in either direction are accessible along the Wales Coast Path. Walkers will find a surplus of footpaths in the surrounding hills and National Trust land.

NA 4 · NP 18 · 16 AMP

WC

Pub, shop, beach and slipway 1 mile.

££££ 🐕 ††

Directions: From Pwllheli, take A497 north sp 'Nefyn'. After 5 miles, turn right at the roundabout adjacent to the Y Bryncynan Inn to stay on A497. Follow A497 into Nefyn and onto B4417 and continue for 1.5 miles. The site is on the left just after the start of the 30mph zone.

GPS: N52°56.897' W004°29.678'
OS grid: 123 SH 324 419

March - October

Gwynt O'r Môr CS

Llanaelhaearn, Caernarfon, LL54 5AY
Tel: 01785 750349
www.gwyntormorcamping.vpweb.co.uk

This mainly sloping site offers beautiful views directly down the valley to the sea. 500m back from the Yr Eifl Mountains create a backdrop with summits up to 564m (1850ft). You can walk 1.5 miles up to Tre'r Ceiri, one of the best preserved and most densely occupied Iron Age hill forts in Britain. There is a café/bar 5 mins walk from the campsite.

NA 0.75 · NP 15 · 10 AMP

WC

Shop 3 miles. Beach and slipway 2 miles.

££££ 🐕 †† M CS

Directions: Turn off A499 onto B4417 at roundabout sp 'Nefyn'. As you enter Llanaelhaearn take the 1st right and the entrance is immediately on the right.

GPS: N52°58.618' W004°24.288'
OS grid: 123 SH 386 449

All year

Aberafon
Camping and Caravan Site

Gyrn Goch, Caernarfon, Gwynedd,
LL54 5PN Tel: 01286 660295
www.aberafon.co.uk

(max 7m)

The location of this site, at the foot of Gyrn Goch Mountain (492m; 1614ft), is delightful with panoramic views and seascapes. There are pitches in a sheltered valley, some on a large field adjacent to and overlooking the sea and some almost on the site's private bathing beach. Nearby there is good sea and river fishing and excellent mountain and coastal walks. Children will find lots to explore and the peaceful atmosphere will keep adults happy too.

| NA | 15 | NP | 65 | 10 AMP | |

| WC | | | | | |

Pub and shop (summer only) 1 mile at Clynnog-Fawr. Slipway on site.

£££

Directions: Located off A499 between Pwllheli and Llanwnda. 1 mile south of Clynnog-Fawr, make a tight turn at a red tin shed into a narrow lane sp for the campsite. The site is at the end of the lane. The turn and the lane to the campsite are not suitable for large caravans or motorhomes.

GPS: N53°00.548' W004°23.166'
OS grid: 123 SH 398 486

April - October

Tan-y-Graig Farm

Penrhosfeilw, Trearddur Bay, Anglesey,
LL65 2LT
Tel: 01407 762043

Located on Holy Island, this small undulating farm site has a sea view from some levelled pitches. In one direction is the South Stack RSPB Reserve and in the other is Trearddur Bay, both a short drive away. The busy ferry port of Holyhead is 1.6 miles where there are pubs, take-aways, banks and a maritime museum. The island's crowning jewel is the ancient church of St Cybi which dates back to 540 AD. The church is located in the town centre inside a three-walled Roman fort.

| NA | 1.5 | NP | 19 | 16 AMP | |

| WC | | | | | |

Pub 2 miles. Beach 0.5 miles. Slipway 2 miles at Trearddur Bay.

£££

Directions: Take A55 to Anglesey and continue to Holyhead. At the roundabout take the 1st exit sp 'Trearddur Bay', then turn immediately right by the pub into Porthdafach Road. Follow this road for 1.5 miles. At the end of the road turn right at the T-junction. The site is on the right in 0.25 miles. The turn into the site is sharp, but longer units can turn around at the next junction.

GPS: N53°17.488' W004°39.708'
OS grid: 123 SH 227 804

April - September

Blackthorn Farm

Penrhos Feilw, Holyhead, Anglesey, LL65 2LT
Tel: 01407 765262
www.blackthornleisure.co.uk

This is a very well appointed site with an elevated position giving a good view to the sea from most pitches. All facilities are of an excellent standard and there is a café, cycle hire and children's entertainment on Saturday mornings during peak season. In one direction is the South Stack RSPB Reserve and the other direction is Trearddur Bay, both a short drive away. The busy ferry port of Holyhead is a mere 1.6 miles away with its restaurants, shops and maritime museum. The island's crowning jewel is the ancient church of St Cybi which dates back to 540 AD. The church is located in the town centre inside a three-walled Roman fort.

| NA 18 | NP 77 | 10 AMP | | |

Pub 2 miles. Slipway 2 miles at Trearddur Bay.

£££ WiFi

Directions: Take A55 to Anglesey and continue to Holyhead. At the roundabout take the 1st exit sp 'Trearddur Bay', then turn immediately right by the pub into Porthdafach Road. Follow this road for 1.5 miles. At the end of the road turn right at the T-junction. The site is on the left in 0.3 miles.

Cymru Wales

GPS: N53°17.531' W004°39.775'
OS grid: 123 SH 225 805

March - October

Penrhyn Bay Caravan Park

Llanfwrog, Anglesey, LL65 4YG
Tel: 01407 730496
www.penrhynbay.com

(max 8m)

This large and level family owned site is located on a small peninsula. Most of the touring pitches are situated around the edge of the site in front of the statics enabling excellent sea views. There is no bar or clubhouse, but there is a heated indoor pool and an all-weather tennis court. There is direct access to a large sandy beach and rocky outcrops that would be good for snorkelling. There is also a sheltered slipway for launching small boats.

| NA 32 | NP 210 | 10 AMP | | |

Pub 4 miles.

£££ WiFi

Directions: Take A55 to Anglesey and exit at Junction 3 following sp 'A5' and 'Y Fali Valley'. After 0.4 miles turn right onto A5025 sp 'Amlwch'. Follow road for 3.25 miles and after the village of Llanfachraeth turn left sp 'Llanfwrog' and 'Penrhyn'. Follow sp 'Penrhyn' and the site is in 2.5 miles at the end of the road.

Cymru Wales

GPS: N53°19.865' W004°34.666'
OS grid: 114 SH 284 846

Easter - October

Ty Newydd CS

Porth Swtan, Church Bay, Anglesey,
LL65 4ET
Tel: 01407 730060

This slightly sloping site is located a mere 160m from the attractive sandy beach at Church Bay and all pitches have sea views. Very close by is the National Trust owned Swtan Cottage as well as a good seafood restaurant and a café. A pub is located up the hill on the far side of the village.

| NA 1 | NP 25 | 10 AMP | | |

| WC | | | | | | MS | MB |

Pub 0.5 miles. Shop 2.5 miles.

££££ 🐕 ♞♞ M CL CS ⓘ WiFi

Directions: Take A55 to Anglesey and exit at Junction 3 following sp 'A5' and 'Y Fali Valley'. After 0.4 miles turn right onto A5025 sp 'Amlwch'. Follow road for 5.75 miles, then turn left in Llanfaethlu sp 'Porth Swtan' and 'Church Bay'. Follow road for 2.5 miles and then turn left sp 'Porth Swtan' and 'Church Bay'. The site is on the left in 120m.

GPS: N53°22.281' W004°33.187'
OS grid: 114 SH 302 890

All year

Gadlys CS

Church Bay, Anglesey, LL65 4ES
Tel: 07786 547361

This small site is located within the Church Bay hamlet of farmsteads. There are good sea views from all pitches. Church Bay's sandy beach is a few mins walk where you will also find a good seafood restaurant, a café, and the National Trust owned Swtan Cottage. A pub is located up the hill in the other direction.

| NA 0.75 | NP 10 | 10 AMP | | |

| WC | | | | | | MS | MB |

Pub 0.5 miles. Shop 2.5 miles.

££££ 🐕 ♞♞ M CL CS ⓘ WiFi

Directions: Take A55 to Anglesey and exit at Junction 3 following sp 'A5' and 'Y Fali Valley'. After 0.4 miles turn right onto A5025 sp 'Amlwch'. Follow road for 6.25 miles, then turn left at 2nd sp for 'Porth Swtan' and 'Church Bay'. Follow road for 2 miles through Rhydwyn, past a pub on the left and down the hill through the village of Church Bay. The site entrance is on the right at a bend in the road.

GPS: N53°22.340' W004°33.096'
OS grid: 114 SH 303 892

April - October

Llanbadrig Vineyard Campsite

Cae Owain, Cemaes Bay, Anglesey,
LL67 0LN
Tel: 01407 710416

Previously part of the now closed Llanbadrig Vineyard, this isolated site isn't much more than a few rough, uneven fields in the hills above Cemaes Bay. However, its elevated position means it offers lovely views over the bay. This is a laidback, extremely basic site where there are no set pitches and open fires are allowed. There are two sandy beaches close by, White Lady Beach is just 0.3 miles and Cemaes main beach is 0.6 miles. The Wales Coast Path runs nearby and you can follow it around the point to the bay and village. Cemaes village, 15 mins direct walk or 5 mins drive, has a shop, several pubs and a fish and chip shop.

NA 2	NP 50	0 AMP		
WC				

££££ 🐕 †† M CL CS ⓘ WiFi

Directions: Take A55 to Anglesey and exit at Junction 8 and follow sp 'Benllech' and 'Amlwch' onto A5025. Follow A5025 for 21.8 miles. Turn right in Neuadd sp 'The Gadlys Country House Hotel'. Continue past the hotel and turn right at the T-junction. Bear right at the next junction and the site entrance is on the right in 0.25 miles. The owner will call to collect payment.

GPS: N53°25.323' W004°26.447'
OS grid: 114 SH 379 944

August plus Bank Holidays

Point Lynas Caravan Park

Llaneilian, Amlwch, Anglesey, LL68 9LT
Tel: 01407 831130
www.pointlynas.co.uk

The view from the camping field takes in the lighthouse at Point Lynas and the sea beyond. The majority of the site is occupied by statics. The tent and motorhome field is partly sloping, but half of the pitches are level. Some of the tent pitches have timber wind breaks which can also serve as drying racks for wetsuits and towels. The facilities are clean and well kept and there is a dog walk and open area for games. The road at the entrance to the site leads 230m to sandy Eilian Cove.

NA 0.75	NP 11	10 AMP		
WC				

Pub and shop 2 miles at Amlwch.

£££ 🐕 †† M CL CS ⓘ WiFi

Directions: Take A55 to Anglesey and exit at Junction 8 and follow sp 'Benllech' and 'Amlwch' onto A5025. Follow A5025 for 15.75 miles. Turn right sp 'Llaneilian' and follow the road for a further 0.9 miles. At the T-junction, turn right sp 'Llaneilian' and the site is 1 mile on the left.

GPS: N53°24.615' W004°17.872'
OS grid: 114 SH 473 928

March - October

Tyddyn Isaf Caravan and Camping Park `101`

Lligwy Bay, Dulas, Anglesey,
LL70 9PQ Tel: 01248 410203
www.tyddynisaf.co.uk

This is a family run, spacious and well laid out hillside site with excellent security. The touring pitches occupy the upper part of the site and most benefit from a fine sea view. There is a large children's play area. Thousands of trees and shrubs have been planted to create a conservation area and haven for wildlife. The site has won numerous quality and conservation awards, including being named AA Campsite of the Year Wales for 2014. The beautiful beach at Lligwy Bay is just 230m away along the site's own private footpath. The Wales Coast Path runs close by and leads 750m to Traeth Dulas Estuary which will fascinate birdwatchers.

| NA 22 | NP 42 | 10/16 AMP | | |

Slipway 2 miles.

£££ 🐕 †† M CL CS ⓘ WiFi

Directions: Take A55 to Anglesey and exit at Junction 8 and follow sp 'Benllech' and 'Amlwch' onto A5025. Follow A5025 for 12 miles. Turn right sp with a campsite symbol and 'Traeth Lligwy'. Turn right and the campsite entrance is 0.5 miles on the right.

Cymru Wales
★★★★★

GPS: N53°21.758' W004°16.535'
OS grid: 114 SH 487 874

Easter - September

Dafarn Rhos Caravan and Camping Site `102`

Lligwy Beach, Moelfre, Anglesey,
LL72 8NN Tel: 01248 410607
www.lligwybeachcampsite.co.uk

A friendly family site with beautiful views over Lligwy Bay. The site is partly sloping, but many pitches are level and many have a sea view. The main toilet and shower facilities are immaculately kept. The beach is 2 mins walk from site through a private access gate. Sometimes seals and their pups, and even dolphins, can be seen close to shore. The Wales Coast Path follows the cliffs both ways, and there is also a designated cycle path that goes past the campsite.

| NA 7.5 | NP 85 | 16 AMP | | |

Pub and shop 1 mile at Moelfre. Slipway 200m.

£££ 🐕 †† M CL CS ⓘ WiFi

Directions: Take A55 to Anglesey and exit at Junction 8 and follow sp 'Benllech' and 'Amlwch' onto A5025. Follow A5025 for 9.75 miles. At the roundabout, turn left to stay on A5025. Turn right after 1.75 miles onto Lôn Traeth Lligwy. Turn left in 0.7 miles sp 'Traeth Lligwy Beach' and the site entrance is on the left in 0.1 miles.

GPS: N53°21.419' W004°15.657'
OS grid: 114 SH 496 868

April - September

Nant Bychan Farm `103`

Moelfre, Anglesey, LL72 8HF
Tel: 01248 410269

This family run farm and campsite is popular with families, many returning every year. The field is partly sloping and there are extensive sea views from all pitches. There is direct access to the rocky shore and a pebbly cove. Alternatively a 10 mins walk along the Wales Coast Path leads you to the sandy beach at Traeth Bychan. Pubs and shops are a few mins walk in the other direction at Moelfre.

`NA` 5   `NP` 35   10 AMP

`WC`   `MG`

Pub, shop and slipway 0.6 miles at Moelfre. Beach 0.2 miles.

££

Directions: Take A55 to Anglesey and exit at Junction 8 and follow sp 'Benllech' and 'Amlwch' onto A5025. Follow A5025 for 9.9 miles. Turn right onto A5108 at the roundabout sp 'Moelfre'. Turn right in 0.5 miles into Ystad Nant Bychan sp 'Camping' and the site is at the end of the road.

GPS: N53°20.922' W004°14.291'
OS grid: 114 SH 513 856

Easter - October

Golden Sunset Camping and Touring Park `104`

Benllech, Anglesey, LL74 8SW
Tel: 0844 5040430
www.goldensunsetholidays.com

This rambling site has extensive camping fields which are separated into large and small enclosures, most of which benefit from excellent sea views. The facilities are quite old but functional. The site is set high on a headland with direct access down to the rocky shore. Benllech is 0.4 miles away and has cafés, restaurants, pubs, and shops. The sheltered sandy beach at Benllech Bay continues on to the large sand and mudflats at Red Wharf Bay. Advanced bookings are not taken except for groups.

`NA` 25   `NP` 70+   10 AMP

`WC`   `MG`

Pub and shop 0.4 miles. Beach and slipway 1 mile.

£££

Directions: Take A55 to Anglesey and exit at Junction 8 and follow sp 'Benllech' and 'Amlwch' onto A5025. Follow A5025 for 8.3 miles. 275m after the Texaco fuel station turn right into the site driveway sp on the fence.

GPS: N53°19.529' W004°13.560'
OS grid: 114 SH 518 832

April - September

St David's Park

Red Wharf Bay, Anglesey, LL75 8RJ
Tel: 01248 852341
www.stdavidspark.com

This camping park is in an outstanding location. The grass touring pitches occupy an enviable position on a small peninsula right on Red Wharf Bay with direct access to the huge beach at low tide. The views across the bay and estuary extend to the east coast of Anglesey and Llandudno's Great Orme clifftop. Onsite facilities are comprehensive and of an excellent standard. The Tavern on the Bay gastropub is adjacent and the historic Ship Inn is 0.5 miles away.

| NA 25 | NP 125 | 16 AMP |

£££

Directions: Take A55 to Anglesey and exit at Junction 8 and follow sp 'Benllech' and 'Amlwch' onto A5025. Follow A5025 for 6.5 miles. Turn right sp 'Red Wharf Bay' and a campsite symbol. Follow sp 'Red Wharf Bay' and the site entrance is straight ahead in 0.5 miles.

Cymru Wales

GPS: N53°18.389' W004°12.687'
OS grid: 114 SH 531 818

March - September

Tyddyn Du Touring Park

Conwy Old Road, Penmaenmawr, LL34 6RE
Tel: 01492 622300
www.tyddyndutouringpark.co.uk

This is a beautifully kept, landscaped and terraced adults only park. There are panoramic views across Conwy Bay to The Great Orme at Llandudno and over to Anglesey and Puffin Island. The campsite has excellent facilities including a well equipped utility/laundry room. Snowdonia National Park is easily accessed with glorious walks for the beginner and enthusiast. An award winning beach is about 15 mins walk. The championship golf course at Conwy is a couple of miles away and Penmaenmawr's delightful golf course is just 200m away.

| NA 5 | NP 100 | 16 AMP |

Pub 90m. Shop 0.5 miles. Beach 0.3 miles. Slipway 1 mile.

£££

Directions: Exit A55 at the large roundabout Junction 16 between Penmaenmawr and Dwygyfylchi sp 'Promenade' with a campsite symbol. Turn immediately left and the site entrance is 275m on the right after The Gladstone pub. Maximum caravan/motorhome length 7.5m (25ft).

Cymru Wales

GPS: N53°16.614' W003°54.289'
OS grid: 115 SH 730 770

March - October

Pendyffryn Farm

Glanyrafon Road, Dwygyfylchi,
Penmaenmawr, Conwy, LL34 6UE
Tel: 01248 681093

This basic site is a large, open, partly sloping field of rough grass with a wide sea view over Conwy Bay. There is an old toilet block on the field which is kept clean. Basic showers and additional toilets are housed in old farm buildings across the road. Open fires are allowed. Behind the site there is a network of hills crisscrossed by footpaths.

| NA | 6 | NP | 100 | 0 AMP | | |

| WC | | | | | | MG | MB |

Pub 0.7 miles. Shop 0.3 miles. Beach 0.2 miles.

££££ | | | M | CL CS | | WiFi

Directions: From east on A55, exit at Junction 16A sp 'Dwygyfylchi'. The site entrance is on the left 180m from the junction. Drive in and pitch, the farmer calls to collect the fees.

GPS: N53°16.898' W003°53.574'
OS grid: 115 SH 738 777

March - October

Pendyffryn Hall
Caravan Park and Country Club

Glanyrafon Road, Dwygyfylchi, Penmaenmawr,
Conwy, LL34 6UF Tel: 01492 623219
www.pendyffrynhall.co.uk

This is a static caravan park with a separate area for tourers and tents. The touring park is mainly level and the tent field is pleasantly located in a secluded valley sheltered by trees. Through the trees campers can enjoy views of the sea. The toilet and shower block has seen better days. Use of the licensed club hall and the adjoining family room is available to campers. The sandy beach at Penmaenmawr is just 10 mins walk and the shops and attractions of Conwy are just 10 mins drive.

| NA | 8 | NP | 65 | 10 AMP | | |

| WC | | | | | | MG | MB |

Pub 0.8 miles. Shop 0.4 miles. Beach 0.2 miles.

£££ | | | M | CL CS | | WiFi

Directions: From east on A55, exit at Junction 16A sp 'Dwygyfylchi'. The site entrance is the 4th entrance on the left, 0.3 miles from the junction.

GPS: N53°16.789' W003°53.590'
OS grid: 115 SH 738 775

March - October

Tan-y-Bryn CS

Bryn Pydew Road, Llandudno Junction,
Conwy, LL31 9JZ
Tel: 01492 549296

This site is set over two mainly sloping fields surrounded by farms and with distant views towards Colwyn Bay and the red roofs of the town. The main field has sloping hardstanding pitches with electric hook-up and there is a separate field for tents. A fridge-freezer is available for campers' use and the shower (£1) is disabled friendly. A steep and narrow 10 mins drive gets you to Conwy.

NA 1.5	NP 20	16 AMP	
WC			

££££ 🐕 †† M CL CS ⓘ WiFi

Directions: Follow A547 into Mochdre and turn onto Station Road and follow over the bridge. At T-junction turn right sp 'Llangwstenin'. Follow for 0.8 miles, then take the left fork going uphill sp 'Pydew'. Follow road for 0.9 miles and the entrance is on the right past the static caravan park of the same name. Large vehicles can continue past the site entrance and turn around at the crossroads.

GPS: N53°17.891' W003°46.944'
OS grid: 116 SH 813 794

All year

Hafodty Farm CL

Hafodty Lane, Colwyn Bay, Conwy, LL28 5YN
Tel: 01492 530161

There is a good view out to Colwyn Bay from this mostly level 1 acre field. There are electric hook-ups and water points, but no toilets or showers. There are walks from the site through hilly countryside to the coast. The seafront at Colwyn Bay is 2 miles away and the Welsh Mountain Zoo is just 1 mile.

NA 1	NP 5	10 AMP	
WC			

Pub and shop 0.5 miles.

££££ 🐕 †† M CL CS ⓘ WiFi

Directions: Exit A55 at Junction 20 onto A547 Conway Road sp 'Mochdre'. Follow sp 'Mochdre' right at the traffic lights, then turn 1st left sp 'Llanrwst B5113'. Follow B5113 sp 'Llanrwst' uphill for 0.9 miles, turning right at a T-Junction. Turn left at the end of the road sp 'Llanrwst B5113'. In 0.3 miles turn right into Mynydd Lane, then turn right into Hafodty Lane. The farm entrance is 100m.

GPS: N53°17.154' W003°44.915'
OS grid: 116 SH 835 780

April - October

Bron-Y-Wendon Touring Park `111`

Wern Road, Llanddulas, Colwyn Bay,
LL22 8HG Tel: 01492 512903
www.bronywendontouringpark.co.uk

This is a top quality, very well kept site with the pitches organised in small groups. All the pitches benefit from beautiful coastal views and the beach is only a short walk away. The long promenade near Llanddulas follows the vast sweep from Old Colwyn to Penrhyn Bay, giving easy access to the wonderful beaches, pier and harbour at Rhos-on-Sea which are all joined by a cycle path. Slipways situated along the promenade provide access for pleasure craft and jet skis. There is some noise from the adjacent railway and A55.

| NA | 8 | NP | 130 | 16 AMP | | |

Pub, shop and beach 0.5 miles. Slipway 3 miles at Colwyn Bay.

££££

Directions: Exit A55 at Junction 23 sp 'Llanddulas'. From east, after exiting turn right and follow road back under A55 sp 'Traeth Beach'. The entrance is on left immediately after the underpass. From west, follow exit road around to left. Site entrance is adjacent to exit road and is well sp with brown campsite/caravan signs.

Cymru Wales ★★★★★

GPS: N53°17.481' W003°38.751'
OS grid: 116 SH 904 785

All Year

Nant Mill Touring Caravan and Tenting Park `112`

Prestatyn, Denbighshire, LL19 9LY
Tel: 01745 852360
www.nantmilltouring.co.uk

This families only site is arranged over four fields, one of which is set aside for tents. From the top row of pitches there is a distant view of the sea which is peppered with wind turbines. Apart from one hardstanding pitch, the site is all grass and partly sloping. It is conveniently situated 0.5 miles from Prestatyn town centre with its bars, restaurants, shops and beach.

| NA | 7 | NP | 150 | 10 AMP | | |

Pub, shop, beach, slipway and children's play area 0.5 miles.

££££

Directions: Adjacent to A548, 0.5 miles east of Prestatyn town centre.

Cymru Wales ★★★★

GPS: N53°20.259' W003°23.598'
OS grid: 116 SJ 073 832

April - October

INDEX

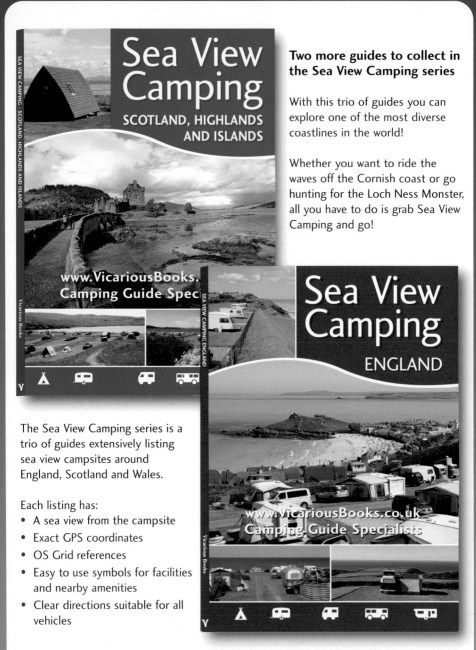

Shell Island

Campfire Cooking

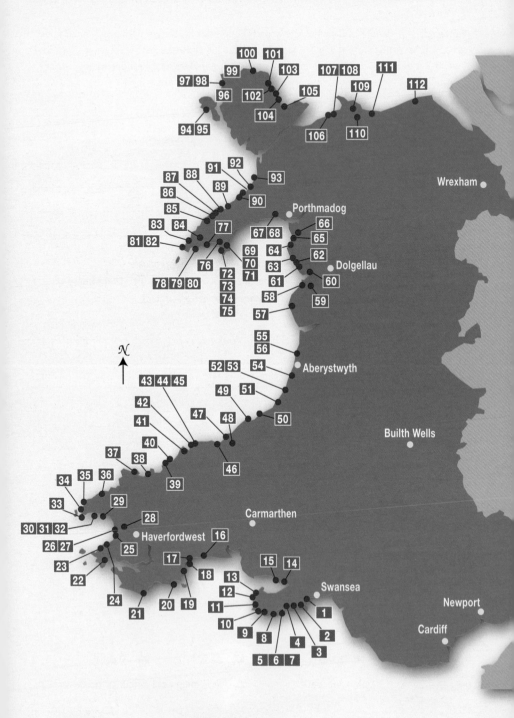

CAMPSITE SUBMISSION FORM

Please use this form to update the site information in this guide. We particularly need good photographs that represent the site and where possible show the sea view. Nominations for new sites are very welcome. If a site is already listed, complete only sections where changes apply. Please fill in answers in capital letters and circle appropriate symbols.

Site Name:

Address:

Postcode:

Tel. No:

Website:

Units accepted by campsite *Please circle 1 or more symbols as appropriate*

Tent   Touring caravan   Motorhome

Large vehicles   Holiday accommodation for hire

Description of site:

NA   Number of acres: NP   Number of pitches:

Electricity available and amperage:

Symbols, facilities *Please circle as appropriate*

Level pitches   All season/hard standing pitches   WC Toilets   Disabled toilets

Showers   Family bathroom/ shower room   Laundry   Dishwashing facilities

MG Motorhome wastewater disposal   MB Motorhome toilet waste disposal

Symbols, amenities *Please circle as appropriate*

Pub/bar   Shop   Beach   Slipway

Children's play area   Footpath   Swimming pool indoor or outdoor

Please see overleaf

CAMPSITE SUBMISSION FORM

Please circle as appropriate

Cost based on two people, one caravan or motorhome with electric in August. Guide prices only.

£	Up to £10 per night	**££**	£10-17 per night	
£££	£17-35 per night	**££££**	£35 or more per night	

🐕	Dogs allowed onsite	**👥**	Adults (Over 18) only	**M**	Members only
CS	Certified Site	*CL*	Certified Location		
ⓘ	Internet available	WiFi	WiFi Available		

Directions to site:

Awards: Cymru Wales star ratings

OS grid references – 1:50,000

GPS Coordinates in the following format: N49°14.988' W000°16.838'

Opening and closing dates:

Photo(s) included: ☐ None ☐ Emailed ☐ Photo(s) posted with form

email pictures to: gomotorhoming@hotmail.co.uk

Name and email or address - so information can be credited:

Please use a separate form for each campsite. Send completed forms to:
Vicarious books, 62 Tontine Street, Folkestone, Kent, CT20 1JP
ask@vicariousbooks.co.uk

Thank you very much for your time.

By supplying details and photographs you are giving unrestricted publication and reproduction rights to Vicarious Books Ltd.

CAMPSITE SUBMISSION FORM

Please use this form to update the site information in this guide. We particularly need good photographs that represent the site and where possible show the sea view. Nominations for new sites are very welcome. If a site is already listed, complete only sections where changes apply. Please fill in answers in capital letters and circle appropriate symbols.

Site Name:

Address:

Postcode:

Tel. No:

Website:

Units accepted by campsite *Please circle 1 or more symbols as appropriate*

Tent   Touring caravan   Motorhome

Large vehicles   Holiday accommodation for hire

Description of site:

NA   Number of acres: NP   Number of pitches:

Electricity available and amperage:

Symbols, facilities *Please circle as appropriate*

Level pitches   All season/hard standing pitches   WC Toilets   Disabled toilets

Showers   Family bathroom/ shower room   Laundry   Dishwashing facilities

MG Motorhome wastewater disposal   MB Motorhome toilet waste disposal

Symbols, amenities *Please circle as appropriate*

Pub/bar   Shop   Beach   Slipway

Children's play area   Footpath   Swimming pool indoor or outdoor

Please see overleaf

CAMPSITE SUBMISSION FORM

Please circle as appropriate

Cost based on two people, one caravan or motorhome with electric in August. Guide prices only.

£   Up to £10 per night   ££   £10-17 per night

£££ £17-35 per night   ££££ £35 or more per night

🐕   Dogs allowed onsite   👫   Adults (Over 18) only   M   Members only

CS   Certified Site   CL   Certified Location

ⓘ   Internet available   [WiFi]   WiFi Available

Directions to site:

....

....

....

....

Awards: Cymru Wales star ratings

....

OS grid references – 1:50,000

....

GPS Coordinates in the following format: N49°14.988' W000°16.838'

....

Opening and closing dates:

Photo(s) included: ☐ None   ☐ Emailed   ☐ Photo(s) posted with form

email pictures to: gomotorhoming@hotmail.co.uk

Name and email or address - so information can be credited:

....

....

Please use a separate form for each campsite. Send completed forms to:

Vicarious books, 62 Tontine Street, Folkestone, Kent, CT20 1JP
ask@vicariousbooks.co.uk

Thank you very much for your time.

By supplying details and photographs you are giving unrestricted publication and reproduction rights to Vicarious Books Ltd.